Contents

Acknowledgements

I am indebted to a number of colleagues in the Hampshire County Council Education Department for their advice and encouragement in the production of this guide. In particular, I would like to record my thanks to Peter Sharp, Assistant Principal Educational Psychologist. He commissioned this work and inspired me, offering helpful advice and guidance throughout the writing and draft stage. Without his help, this book would not have been possible and that I warmly acknowledge.

I would also like to thank other colleagues within and beyond the Educational Psychology Service, particularly Rob Mason who gave unselfishly of his time to proof read and comment on one draft and to Pamela Belbin, my secretary, for patiently putting the professional touches to my manuscript.

In this guide, I have quoted from the Code of Practice and made reference to other publications from the Department for Education. Crown copyright is reproduced with kind permission of the Controller of Her Majesty's Stationery Office. Other copyright material is reproduced with permission from the publishers. I have also used ideas from teachers and other colleagues, including material on Individual Education Plans generously given to me by Gill Tester, Special Needs Inspector. To everyone who has assisted me, please accept my grateful thanks.

Finally, I would like to record my appreciation and gratitude to my family and friends for 'putting up' with me whilst I was glued to my computer.

Ahmad F Ramjhun
Educational Psychologist
Hampshire County Council Education Department
August 1995

IMPLEMENTING THE CODE OF PRACTICE FOR CHILDREN WITH
SPECIAL EDUCATIONAL NEEDS

A Practical Guide

AHMAD F. RAMJHUN

David Fulton Publishers
London
in association with
Hampshire County Council

David Fulton Publishers Ltd
2 Barbon Close, London WC1N 3JX

First published in Great Britain by
David Fulton Publishers 1995
Reprinted 1996

British Library Cataloguing in Publication Data

A catalogue record for this book is available from the British Library

ISBN 1-85346-416-3

Typeset by The Harrington Consultancy
Printed in Great Britain by Bell & Bain Ltd., Glasgow

Foreword

The 1993 Education Act was a huge legislative task which, in the end, involved 622 government amendments. The sections on special needs range, however, from acceptable to excellent.

Some Secretaries of State have treated consultation of people with knowledge and expertise with disdain, the Code of Practice has been an exception. It has succeeded in balancing divergent interests and providing clear guidance.

Whilst the legislation and guidance are helpful by recent standards, the task set for schools and LEAs is formidable. From the earliest drafts of the Code, and in keeping with their normal commitment to children and schools, conscientious LEA staff have devoted long hours to understanding and implementing these matters. We have briefed each other, shared experience and expertise and helped governors and staff in schools understand and apply the requirements of the 1993 Act and the Code of Practice.

To some extent we have all been inventing wheels. Whilst some local interpretation is essential I know this book will help specialists and non-specialists alike. Ahmad's work in Hampshire has been far wider than assessing children and advising parents and schools (though that is wide enough!) and he has drawn on that experience in a way that makes this book an accessible and useful document for all kinds of reader. Whether you are an enquirer or consider yourself an expert this book will simplify the task of understanding and will assist implementation.

Peter Coles
County Education Officer
Hampshire County Council
August 1995

Preface

Education in this country has been subject to fierce and rapid changes over the past decade. Claims have been made about 'falling standards' in spite of the lack of evidence and political attempts made to put right the perceived inadequacies in the system. This started with the now famous 'Ruskin' speech made by James Callaghan in 1986, followed by various legislation to centralise control (see Evans and Tomlinson, 1989). Teachers have borne the brunt of the criticisms, not all justified or warranted, being seen to have failed to raise standards and to prepare children for their future role as citizens and providers for the nation. There followed attempts, some well intentioned and others misguided, to grasp control over schools and to determine the education provided to children (Booth, 1989; Galloway et al, 1994).

Central government assumed control of the curriculum, resulting in the imposition of a National Curriculum to be followed by all state schools and prescribed in great detail, initially with little room for teachers and others responsible for its implementation to manoeuvre. Legislation in the form of the 1988 Education Act was passed by the Conservative government, requiring the study of core subjects by all children and prescribing standard assessments at key stages of children's schooling, i.e at 7, 11, 14 and 16. Considerable controversy ensued, amidst resistance from the teacher unions, forcing a reconsideration of the issues and the tasks expected of teachers. The end result has been a slimmed down version of the National Curriculum and increased teacher flexibility in recognition of their responsibilities and superior knowledge of the child in their class (see the Dearing Report, 1994).

Children with special educational needs have also been the subject of detailed attention, resulting in far reaching changes in the way they are viewed and educated. The Warnock Report on the Education of Children with Special Educational Needs (1978) inspired new thinking and a radically different approach to the concept of special need. Children were no longer to be categorised into groups for learning difficulties and the focus was no longer on their disability. Rather, the emphasis was on children's needs and the help they require to make progress in their learning.

The 1981 Education Act incorporated the recommendations of the Warnock Committee. The Act was not implemented in local education authorities (LEAs) until April 1983 and has had a mixed reception amongst schools, LEAs, parents and central government. Its Achilles heel was the cost to education providers and the number of appeals that arose through conflict from perceived inadequacies to provide for children in need. It was therefore inevitable that it would be revised and repealed by new legislation. This came about in the form of the 1993 Education Act, much of which concentrates on Grant Maintained Status for schools. Part 3, however, is specifically concerned with the education of children with special educational needs. This details the requirements of the assessment and review procedures and requires the provision of a Code of

Practice to provide guidance to LEAs, Health Trusts, Social Services Departments and schools on how to discharge their responsibilities with regard to children with special educational needs.

The Code of Practice is a comprehensive document, approved by Parliament in 1994. It came into effect in September 1994 and all parties in education are required to have regard to its guidance. It should be remembered that the Code is the result of legislation and is pursuant to the 1993 Education Act. Therefore, it ought to be read widely and to be understood by teachers and others who are closely affected by its guidance and requirements.

This book on the implementation of the Code of Practice arises from a perceived need for teachers, LEA officers, governors and parents and the voluntary agencies to have a practical and accessible guide to help them discharge their key duties and responsibilities. It was commissioned by the Hampshire Educational Psychology Service, following a number of requests from schools and other agencies for training in relation to their duties and responsibilities, in addition to the new procedures and practices arising from the Code. It therefore represents an attempt to identify the key issues and to provide guidance on the requirements. The core of the text is written primarily with teachers and education support staff in mind, though parents, governors and staff from both statutory and voluntary agencies will find the contents equally useful.

Chapter 1 starts with an overview of the Code, and Chapter 2 details its implications for the class teacher in primary and secondary schools. Chapter 3 is more focused on the roles of Governing Bodies and includes guidance on the preparation of schools' special educational needs policies. Chapter 4 deals with the preparation of Individual Education Plans (IEPs) and provides guidance on their preparation and completion, including a section on a selection of problem solving strategies which teachers may find useful. Chapter 5 deals with the Stages of the Code and details the process, requirements and responsibilities at each stage. Chapter 6 describes the statutory process and discusses criteria for statutory assessment, including guidance on how to prepare the Educational Advice (called the Appendix D). Chapters 7 and 8 concentrate on the Annual Review procedures and the Transition Plan which is produced for a student at 14+ years of age. Chapter 9 deals with parents rights, roles and responsibilities and includes a section on the Special Educational Needs Tribunal.

A recurring theme throughout the book is the need to ascertain and include the child's perspective, in addition to the views of the parents. Parents are also encouraged to include the views of the family where this is relevant. It is firmly held that the starting point with any teaching activity should be the child, whether or not the child has special needs. Every child is different, so there is no panacea or cure all; the advice is know your child and do not assume that problems that appear similar are the same. Much will depend on the creativity and insight of the teacher but no progress will be made until and unless the child is actively engaged. This implies a number of requirements, amongst which the most important are to gain the child's trust and confidence, to build and develop a mutually satisfying relationship and to enable co-operation. If parents are also brought in as active partners, this makes for a more effective and planned approach, ensuring consistency and coherence which can only be to the good.

The convention adopted in this book is to use the masculine 'he' when referring to a child. This is in order to avoid the cumbersome usage of he/she to refer to children and no discrimination is intended in any way.

This book is not intended to be other than a practical guide to the Code of Practice. The only authoritative version is the Code itself which has Parliamentary approval. Therefore, reference should be made to the Code for specific guidance where doubts exist or to the 1993 Education Act and the associated regulations for points of law. The views expressed in this work are the author's and do not necessarily represent those of Hampshire County Council.

I hope this book guides you through the effective implementation of the Code of Practice.

Disclaimer

The examples given as case studies in this work are purely fictitious and are provided for the purpose of illustration only. Any resemblance to any person is purely coincidental.

Purpose

The purpose of this handbook is to enable the reader to:

* understand and implement the requirements of the Code of Practice with regard to children with special educational needs

* discharge their duties and responsibilities at each stage of their work and with specific reference to the Code

* follow best practice in working with and supporting children with special educational needs

Audience

This handbook is intended as a resource for:

* teachers and special needs assistants in schools, whether or not they work directly with a child with special educational needs

* headteachers and special needs co-ordinators whose task is to ensure implementation and facilitation of the Code in their schools

* governing bodies whose responsibilities are to ensure that their schools are having regard to the Code

* LEA officers, psychologists, health and social services staff who have a part to play in the implementation of the Code

* parents who will also find this handbook useful in identifying the duties placed on schools and others when providing for their child with special educational needs. It will help clarify the roles and responsibilities of the various staff who work with their children, the procedures to be followed and the documentation to be kept; it will also help them to understand their role when working in partnership with the various agencies

Overview

Each chapter sets out to answer the following questions:

What is the Code of Practice about? (*Chapter 1*)
As a member of staff in a school, what do I need to know and do? (*Chapter 2*)
As a governor, what do I need to know and do? (*Chapter 3*)
How are good IEPs produced? (*Chapter 4*)
What do I need to know about the Stages in the Code? (*Chapter 5*)
How do I get through the maze called 'statutory assessment'? (*Chapter 6*)
How do I make the best of the Annual Review? (*Chapter 7*)
How do I write a good Transition Plan? (*Chapter 8*)
What do I as a parent need to know about the Code? (*Chapter 9*)

List of abbreviations

ACE	Advisory Centre for Education
AT	Attainment Target
CMO	Clinical Medical Officer or School Doctor
DES	Department of Education and Science
DFE	Department for Education
EP	Educational Psychologist
FEFC	Further Education Funding Council
IEP	Individual Education Plan
LEA	Local Education Authority
NC	National Curriculum
NVQ	National Vocational Qualification
OFSTED	Office for Standards in Education
PEST	A problem solving technique which examines the political, economic, social and technological aspects of problems/issues
QTA	Qualified Teacher Assistance
SEN	Special Educational Needs
SENCO	SEN Co-ordinator
SNA	Special Needs Assistant
STA	Specialist Teacher Adviser (for a type of learning difficulty)
SWOT	Strengths, Weaknesses, Opportunities and Threats analysis

CHAPTER 1

An Introduction to the Code of Practice

Introduction to handbook

This handbook is intended for teachers, parents and LEA officers with an interest in the education of children with special educational needs (SEN). It summarises the Code of Practice and details its implications for parents, teachers, non-teaching assistants and other professionals closely involved in supporting the education of all children within and beyond school.

The premise on which this handbook is based is that any complex activity requires sound planning, purposeful action, careful monitoring through systematic records and objective evaluation. The Code emphasises this need in teaching and calls for a cycle of planning, assessment and review. This is the minimum requirement, especially with children whose learning needs are severe and complex, requiring a rigorous approach in the education they receive. In these cases, the task of responding effectively to the children's needs calls for an understanding of what these needs are, and systematic planning as to the necessary teaching and action. This is followed by evaluation of any intervention or programme used. Such an approach focuses on the actions and creativity of the teacher, without involving the need to attribute learning responses and/or failures to factors 'within the child'. Thus, there is no blame attached to the child's innate ability, disposition or other circumstances, the responsibility being very much on the parent or teacher whose task is to take account of all relevant factors that may be having an effect on learning and to include these in their intervention.

This handbook does not propose to cover the requirements of the Code in detail as this is best done by reading the Code itself. Instead what follows is a translation of some of the key requirements into practical guidance for teachers and others. The focus is on what the Code means to parents, teachers, governors and other staff with direct responsibility for children's learning. This includes discussions of the kind of expectations which can be reasonably made and the procedures to be followed in order to 'have regard to the Code' and fulfil its requirements. Guidelines on how to prepare Individual Education

Plans (IEPs) are included, together with some suggested proformas. There is also a chapter on how to prepare for meetings, particularly those dealing with Annual Reviews and the preparation of the Transition Plan at post 14 years of age.

The Code of Practice: an overview

The Code of Practice came into effect in September 1994. It is a requirement of the 1993 Education Act, calling on the Secretary of State to provide practical guidance to Local Education Authorities (LEAs), schools and other agencies, namely Social Services Departments and Health Trusts, on how to discharge their responsibilities with regard to children who have special educational needs.

The Code represents a significant milestone in special needs thinking and provides detailed and comprehensive guidance on:

- the procedures to be followed on the identification and assessment of children who have special educational needs;
- the planning, teaching and provision to meet those needs;
- the responsibilities of LEAs, schools, Health Services and Social Services Departments, to work in partnership with each other and with parents, in their responses to children with special educational needs.

It provides a framework to inform and support practices to help children with special educational needs and builds on the principles first set out in the 1981 Education Act. In common with other legislation, e.g. the National Curriculum, it includes a certain amount of prescription, particularly with regard to procedures, but leaving some flexibility with the processes – for example, in relation to formal criteria for statutory assessment, and schools' decisions on their special educational needs policies, allocation of special educational needs resources and organisational arrangements.

There are clear and specific expectations, some setting out precisely the stages to be followed in assessment and minimum requirements relating to matters such as consultation with parents and involvement of outside agencies. Other requirements are more focused on the need for prompt and effective response within statutory time limits, especially on:

- the statutory assessment of children, LEAs being required to complete the process within 26 weeks;
- the procedures relating to Annual Reviews;
- parental rights and expectations and in particular
- the time to be allowed for parents to study reports, professional advice and/or evidence prior to Annual Reviews;
- the time limits between 14+ reviews and the receipt of Transition Plans.

The Code, however, is not explicit on criteria for statutory assessment and asserts that indeed it could not be, these being matters for individual LEAs to decide. This could be a potential area of misunderstanding and conflict but if the framework offered by the Code is strictly followed, with responsibilities emphasised at the school level, a hierarchy of stages and needs could be established providing the necessary documentation and evidence forming part of the criteria.

The Code represents best practice in relation to the assessment and support of children with special educational needs. It also has many resource implications which will require careful and effective responses, especially in the current political and economic climate when resources are so scarce. With local management of schools, the responsibility for deployment of these resources rests with schools and their governing bodies as a substantial number of children with special educational needs will be expected to be supported from funds already delegated to them. This is because the Code reinforces the following key assumptions and requirements:

1. Twenty per cent of children are likely to have a special educational need at some time in their school career. The majority will be educated in the mainstream, with a very small number (2 per cent) provided with a Statement of Special Educational Needs.

2. All children with special educational needs, i.e. all of the 20 per cent, will have their needs met. This means specific, targeted resources to support these children, with documentation to provide evidence of the necessary planning, consultation and teaching.

3. Specific staff will undertake responsibility for the provision required by children with special educational needs, ranging from the nominated 'responsible person' to the special educational needs co-ordinator and special educational needs teams in larger schools.

If, as expected, more children attract support and stay in the mainstream, without a statement, schools will have to allocate their resources as efficiently as possible, given the increased demands imposed on staff by the Code's new procedures, e.g. IEP meetings, preparation of paperwork, consultation with parents. There is also the challenge of ensuring that suitably qualified and experienced staff are available to implement the appropriate learning programmes, in addition to supporting the ordinary class teacher. Consideration will therefore need to be given to in-service training and other requirements of the teaching and non-teaching staff.

Background to the Code of Practice

It can be said that the Code of Practice was introduced in order to put right some of the deficiencies which have been perceived to have arisen since the implementation of the 1981 Education Act. Most notable of these are the criticisms which have been made by the Audit Commission in their reports: *Getting in on the Act* and *Getting the Act Together* (Audit Commission/HMI, 1992a and 1992b). These are:

- lack of accountability by some schools in their use of resources allocated for children with special educational needs.

  – The main problem here was that some schools failed to specify exactly how resources had been targeted to support children with special educational needs. Conspicuous among this was an absence of details relating to teaching programmes and their organisation and implementation, including the staff allocation needed.

- unacceptably long delays by LEAs to process the statutory assessment of children with special educational needs.

  - The Audit Commission found that the majority of LEAs were taking far too long to complete the statutory assessment procedures, under the terms of the 1981 Education Act. This ranged from a few months to a few years, revealing inconsistencies between LEAs and raising suspicion amongst parents and pressure groups that the procedures were being used as delaying tactics.

- the making of statements of special educational needs which were too vague, lacking in specificity and clarity relating to objectives and provision, making these weak and potentially liable to abuse.

  - This is a common observation, particularly from the recipients of statements, and also reinforced by the Audit Commission. The main criticisms have been that the child's special educational needs have tended, on the whole, not to be clearly specified. There were occasionally failures to specify each and every need (i.e. the 'Dorset judgment', 1991) and a lack of specificity relating to the provision needed, including some confusion as to exactly *who* should be funding specialist resources, such as speech therapy (i.e. the 'Oxford judgment'). (See Denman and Lunt, 1993, for a review of cases which have gone to judicial review.)

- the increase in the number of appeals reaching the Secretary of State and the perceived need to bring consistency and fairness in regard to Appeal Committees' recommendations, leading to their replacement with the new Special Educational Needs Tribunals.

  - The main concern here was the inability of the Appeals Committees to enforce their recommendations on LEAs, as the latter could choose to ignore them – leaving the only recourse for the parents being to appeal to the Secretary of State. This was compounded no doubt by the lack of consistency of Appeal Committees; and, the possible role conflict of county councillors sitting on them, the conflicting roles being loyalty to their LEAs as elected representatives and their obligation to safeguard the best interests of the child. This raised doubts about objectivity and impartiality (Chasty and Friel, 1991; Robinson, 1994; DFE, 1994).

It was therefore inevitable that legislation would be undertaken in an attempt to resolve these issues. Part III of the 1993 Education Act tries to address these concerns. This it did by repealing most of the 1981 Education Act and by making specific provisions for each of the above, including the requirement for a Code of Practice to be produced to secure practical guidance to LEAs and others with responsibility for children with special educational needs (see Robinson, 1994).

Fundamental principles of the Code of Practice

The Code is firmly based on the following principles which are intended to influence and guide planning and action in providing for children with special educational needs. These are:

- a child's right to an education in the mainstream;
- a child's entitlement to a broad and balanced curriculum, including the National Curriculum;
- the entitlement of *all* children with special educational needs to have their needs addressed, including a recognition of the continuum of needs to be matched with a continuum of provision;
- the rights of pre-schoolers with special educational needs and the need for early and effective intervention;
- active partnership within and between agencies, with the close involvement of parents;
- accountability, efficiency and effectiveness at all stages.

The aims of the Code of Practice

The aims of the Code are to:

multi-agency

- help schools and other responsible agencies make effective decisions on how to fulfil their responsibilities with regard to children with special educational needs;
- obtain best value from resources targeted at children with special educational needs;
- ensure the matching of provision to need through a five stage model of assessment;
- improve practice in schools and in the classroom by

  - ensuring early screening, identification and reporting of learning difficulties
  - thorough and progressively more detailed assessments in respect of children's learning difficulties
  - requiring that identified learning difficulties lead to prompt planning and intervention
  - requiring the keeping of clear and systematic records to enable the monitoring and evaluation of a child's progress
  - enabling records to be used at information giving, planning and decision making meetings, e.g. informal meetings with parents, agreeing IEPs, Annual Reviews, Transition Plan meetings
  - identifying key responsibilities for best practice in schools for children with special educational needs;

- encourage parents and teachers to seek help to improve their best endeavours with children;
- give children a voice by

  - requiring that children and their parents are consulted in decision making, whenever possible and appropriate
  - encouraging both children's and their parents' views to be recorded in statutory and other documentation;

- make LEAs, Health and Social Services more accountable to parents by

  - ensuring that statutory assessments are completed on time and

5

within specified limits
– the setting up of Special Educational Needs Tribunals to resolve disputes.

New requirements

The Code introduces a number of new requirements, the most important of which are listed below:

● children have a right to make their views known; they should be listened to and be encouraged to participate in decision making;

● schools must maintain a register of all children with special educational needs and publish their Special Educational Needs Policy, detailing the arrangements for the children and the people responsible;

● special educational needs co-ordinators should ensure that an Individual Education Plan (IEP) is drawn up for all pupils from Stage 2 onwards;

● parents should have the support of a 'named person', who can offer advice and information; such a person should be independent of the LEA;

● a Transition Plan is to be drawn up for children who are aged 14 or over to prepare for the transition from school to adult life; this replaces the statutory re-assessment (at the age of $13\frac{1}{2}$ to $14\frac{1}{2}$) under previous legislation;

● statements of special educational needs must detail precisely the needs of the child and the educational requirements, including broad objectives;

● parents are to have access to a quick and independent system of appeal at Special Educational Needs Tribunals (but see Chapter 9); these are to be non-departmental public organisations, completely independent of local and central government;

● LEAs are to have regard to the Code; when disputes arise, Special Educational Needs Tribunals will be specifically concerned with whether or not they have made the right decision in the particular circumstances;

● OFSTED inspections are to consider the effectiveness of school policies and practices in the light of the Code.

Conclusion

There are significant implications arising from the Code relating to everybody actively engaged in supporting children with special educational needs. Whilst the Code does not have the full force of law, all parties are required, under the 1993 Education Act, 'to have regard' to its provisions. There are many procedures to think about and processes to be gone through. These range from the planning of IEPs to the conduct of Annual Reviews and the preparation of Transition Plans.

The main objective, however, is to ensure that *all* children receive the most efficient education possible. This implies a degree of accountability in teachers and other professionals whose contribution may be evaluated against the Code's provisions with regard to best practice.

CHAPTER 2

Implications for the class teacher

Definition of special educational needs

The Code adopts the definition of special educational needs as laid down in the 1981 Education Act and subsequently in the 1993 Education Act.

A child has special educational needs if he or she has a learning difficulty which calls for special educational provision to be made for him or her.

A child has a learning difficulty if he or she:

(a) has a significantly greater difficulty in learning than the majority of children of the same age
(b) has a disability which either prevents or hinders the child from making use of educational facilities of a kind provided for children of the same age in schools within the area of the local educational authority
(c) is under five and falls within the definition at (a) or (b) above or would do if special educational provision was not made for the child.

A child must not be regarded as having a learning difficulty solely because the language or form of language of the home is different from the language in which he or she is or will be taught.

Special educational provision means:

(a) for a child over two, educational provision which is additional to, or otherwise different from, the educational provision made generally for children of the child's age in maintained schools, other than special schools, in the area
(b) for a child under two, educational provision of any kind.

(Section 156)

Source: Code of Practice, HMSO 1994

The concept of special educational needs appears to be conditional on the existence of a learning difficulty which is defined in (a) to (c) above. These definitions have direct implications for teachers and other education providers, impinging directly on accepted practice and beliefs. Each of these is examined in turn below.

(a) *A child has a learning difficulty if he or she has a significantly greater difficulty in learning than the majority of children of the same age*

The words 'significantly greater difficulty in learning' are of the essence here. How this is arrived at in practice is certainly subject to individual variation, though it is likely to be interpreted as performance which falls below the bottom 2 per cent of the child's age group.

Teachers might compare the child's performance on such measures as in the following sections 1 to 5.

1. *National Curriculum Attainments* – especially the discrepancy between the achievements of the 'average' child in a particular year group and those of the child with special educational needs.

Teachers could prepare a list of the attainments of children in their class and make a simple frequency count, i.e. how many are achieving at the levels of the National Curriculum. For example, out of a group of 50 eleven year olds, there may be 25 achieving at Level 3, 15 working towards Level 3 and 10 still working towards Level 2, one of whom is working within Level 1. Changing these figures into percentages would lead to the following:

Percentage	National Curriculum Level
50	Level 3
30	Towards Level 3
18	Towards Level 2
2	Within Level 1

Frequency counts can be maintained for individual classes and year groups and aggregated to provide percentages for the whole school. These provide norms, the idea being that the bottom 20 per cent and especially the 2 per cent, will attract funding from the school's special educational needs budget to provide the help required. Children in the 20 per cent can be followed up and placed in the appropriate Stages for help. Those in the bottom 2 per cent can then be considered for intensive support and, if need be, for recommendation to the LEA for statutory assessment.

In the example above, the average 11 year old is achieving at Level 3, i.e. the standard reached by 50 per cent of the children in that year group. Eighty per cent are achieving or working towards Level 3, with only 20 per cent working towards Level 2. Out of this 20 per cent, 2 per cent are *significantly underachieving*.

2. *Results of reading, spelling or number assessments* – perhaps centiles from reading/spelling ages.

Standardised tests are useful in that they provide norms in relation to reading/spelling ages. However, these should be used cautiously and interpreted in context. Teachers should also incorporate their own assessments from their knowledge of the child, e.g. his style of learning and progress over time. The latter information is very useful and pertinent, making up for deficiencies which are intrinsic to standardised assessments. For example, children may score at very low levels in a standardised reading or spelling assessment which is focusing on accuracy but may be developing the necessary phonic or other word attack skills they are being taught. These are more relevant to teaching and the child's needs and normally such discrepancies should cause no surprise or concern to parents and others if the value and reliability of standard assessments are in question. Similarly, many children are able to read fluently but with little understanding of meaning, thereby masking their difficulties.

3. *Profiles of achievement in different areas of the curriculum*

Forming a profile of the child's achievements is an extremely useful process. This normally serves to indicate the child's abilities and needs, highlighting problem areas as well as those which could be used to boost the child's confidence and self-esteem. Psychologists often find that a child who was initially thought to be of low ability because of low academic attainments may be functioning at average levels or more. However, they fail to achieve in a particular area which depresses their overall attainments and makes them appear to be less able than they are. This is the case with children who have a specific learning difficulty, perhaps in reading and/or spelling. Their work may show significant weaknesses and they may also be experiencing difficulties with access to the literacy components of the curriculum. In these cases, it is useful to draw up a profile which shows the child's cognitive strengths and weaknesses. This helps with planning, such as which area to address within teaching, the kinds of material and approaches which are more likely to ensure effective access to the curriculum, and the teaching of compensatory strategies.

4. *The child's behaviour and learning*

It is a truism that a happy, well settled child is able to devote more time and energy to his learning compared with one with a variety of worries and anxieties, not all immediate or obvious. Consequently, teachers should be alert to signs of children not applying themselves, seeming unable to concentrate or to persevere with tasks. A measure of their concentration span or work output is often helpful as are observations focusing on interactions with peers, teachers and other adults. Other useful indices relate to:

- *Communication patterns* Does the child show a desire to communicate? Or does he avoid or resist encouragement to do so? Does the child maintain or avoid eye contact? Does he take turns or are communications one way?
- *Communication contents* – maturity of language, repetition of words, ideas, extent of vocabulary, information content, sentence construction, clarity of speech sounds.
- *Level of understanding* – including development of listening skills.
- *Personal skills* – relating to self help and independence, e.g. dressing, eating, washing, toileting.
- *Personal safety* – road sense, conformity to norms and conventions, e.g. not climbing/sitting or jumping out of windows, not wandering, going with strangers.
- *Physical needs* – mobility, sight, hearing, gross and fine motor skills.

5. *Other factors relevant to the child's learning*

The majority of children are in caring, supportive families, concerned for their welfare, happiness, development and education. Others may not be so fortunate (see Rutter and Madge, 1981). It is therefore crucial that teachers are aware of and take into account the child's individual circumstances, particularly:

• the level of help and support available from the immediate family, parents or carers;

• the facilities for study and self-development which families can or cannot afford;

• any experiences of care or changes of care outside of the immediate family, including any future changes pending;

• any event or incident which is likely to have a significant impact on the child, e.g. a bereavement, experiences of abuse or the diagnosis of a critical illness in the child or other members of the family; separation of the parents or divorce are also likely to cause tensions and affect the child's emotional readiness for learning.

(b) *A disability which either prevents or hinders the child from making use of educational facilities of a kind provided for children of the same age in schools within the area of the local education authority*

This could mean a physical or sensory disability, e.g. lack of mobility, hearing or visual impairment, but could also include other difficulties, such as:

• an emotional or social difficulty which makes it impossible for the child to work co-operatively with his teachers or his peers;

• a combination of needs which require provision different from or exceeding those normally provided in schools, e.g. a profoundly disabled child with physical, sensory and severe learning difficulties.

(c) *Child is under five and falls within the definition at (a) or (b) above or would do if special educational provision was not made for the child*

This relates to pre-school children who have needs as described in (a) and (b) above, which require early and structured intervention. This could be provided of course in a nursery, language or other units, or even in nursery classes of infant schools where these are established.

Children whose home language is different from the language of instruction

The Code repeats previous advice that a child must not be regarded as having a learning difficulty on the sole basis that their language is different from the language of instruction in school. Bilingualism is an asset and should be recognised as such.

There is therefore a particular need for caution in the type of assessments to be used with these children, especially for these to:

• be culture free and culture fair as far as is possible;

• include results relating to performance which are not directly influenced or affected by lack of English, e.g. non-verbal tests.

Implications for the class teacher

The Code makes significant requirements on all teachers, irrespective of whether or not they have responsibility for special educational needs. All teachers are, of course, teachers of special educational needs and in a sense, it is true to say that when a child has these needs, so does the teacher. This is because of the special care and planning required to ensure that learning progresses.

The Code formalises this process of planning. Though teachers have always planned and maintained records, this is now a requirement in the form of the Individual Education Plans. Therefore, irrespective of the stage reached by the child under the Code's procedures, all class teachers need to have regard to the provision and they may need to adjust their practice to meet the requirements. There is no difference either at pre- or post-statutory stage, except that the child with more significant needs is likely to require more detailed planning and responses. The implications for the teacher at each stage are outlined below but there should be no assumption that the processes are separate and distinct, only that the requirements at the post-statutory stages are likely to be higher.

Pre-statutory stage

The class teacher needs to demonstrate that:

1. All the required stages have been followed, with appropriate documentation completed over a period of time.
2. Parents have been consulted at an early stage and regular communication maintained with them.
3. A number of strategies have been tried to help the child, carefully planned and under the close supervision of the teacher, including consultation with the special educational needs co-ordinator.

This means:
   (a) Setting clear objectives
   (b) Monitoring progress on a regular basis
   (c) Consulting, if in doubt, normally with the special educational needs co-ordinator
   (d) Reviewing objectives and progress and setting new targets
   (e) Working within specified time frames

4. Individual Education Plans are being maintained and worked to.

Post-statutory stage

The class teacher needs to demonstrate that he or she is:

1. Fully conversant with the contents and requirements of the Statement.
2. Working to the requirements through clearly stated objectives within planned and systematic programmes.
3. Doing all of that listed in 1 to 4 under the heading 'Pre-statutory stage', and able to:
   (a) Plan and contribute to the Annual Review
   (b) Provide accurate and detailed information as and when required
   (c) Answer questions from parents and other parties and be able to produce the evidence on the rare occasions when challenged
   (d) Defend a particular approach or point of view at a Special Educational Needs Tribunal if necessary.

Action for teachers

1. Make sure parents know what you are doing, rather than just your concerns.

2. Enlist their help and make it clear that you wish to work in partnership with them, sharing responsibility for the task of helping their child.

3. Consult with your special educational needs co-ordinator and keep them in touch with the work that you are doing.

4. Keep full and clear records.

5. Do not show any unease, and speak with confidence, at meetings and Annual Reviews, armed with the facts about the child's learning. Remember that you are the only person with direct and daily contact with the child and therefore know as much as and probably more than anyone else.

6. Come to meetings prepared, with all the necessary records and programmes. You are likely to be asked about:
   - National Curriculum Attainments (and their meanings to parents)
   - Reading/spelling/writing attainments
   - Number skills
   - Factors affecting learning in the classroom.

7. Show that you have planned and made arrangements to enhance learning in the classroom (crucially for all children including the child with special needs).

8. Know about, accumulate and use the appropriate material with children who have learning difficulties. This is one of the areas in which your special educational needs co-ordinator is a useful resource.

9. Discuss problems and concerns early and keep everybody informed, not forgetting your headteacher and special educational needs co-ordinator.

10. Set yourself objectives which are SMART:

    S – Simple

    M – Measurable

    A – Achievable

    R – Realistic

    T – Translatable into teaching terms

11. Follow the cycle of:

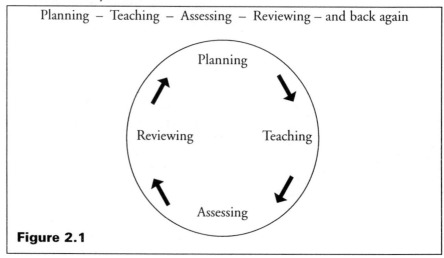

Planning – Teaching – Assessing – Reviewing – and back again

Figure 2.1

Implementation of the Code of Practice in secondary schools

Secondary schools offer a context which is different and organisationally more complex to that existing in primary schools. There are more staff, tighter timetabling constraints, more complex curricular and organisational arrangements, which all have to be taken account of in planning for the child with special needs. Ordinarily, a great deal of the organising and responsibility falls on the special educational needs co-ordinator and most schools have special needs departments which serve as bases and points of reference for children, parents and staff alike.

The difference between primary and secondary schooling is that the child in the secondary school is taught by many more teachers, as opposed to just the one or the very few they were used to before. The former tend to be subject specialists and may not be able to see or teach the child for more than a few lessons per week. This normally means that they need longer to get to know the child, perhaps able to form impressions about performance in their subject area but without a complete view of the whole child in his functioning. Consultation and co-operation within and between subject areas is, therefore, likely to produce dividends, as it is interesting to see how the child is working in areas different to one's own. This may at minimum mean no more than comparing notes or reading subject reports on a child who is causing concern, though co-operative planning and active collaboration will be necessary for more severe problems, e.g. the child who is disruptive in lessons or who is truanting.

The Stages of the Code of Practice apply to the secondary schoolteacher in the same way as they do in primary schools. However, there are some essential differences.

Roles and responsibilities of subject teachers

1. Stage 1 may show a variety and range of responses from subject specialists which then need to be organised to form an overview of the child.

Subject teachers' responsibilities are to provide a clear picture of how the child is functioning in their class and in particular:

- how he is dealing and coping with the requirements;
- an indication of the child's attitude, interest, disposition and application to learning in their particular subject area;
- the child's performance and how this compares with that of his peers and what would normally be expected;
- the arrangements that are having to be made to accommodate the child's difficulties.

Such information need not be too detailed at Stage 1 as the purpose is to collate and compare teachers' views and observations of children causing concern, with a view to clarifying the nature of that concern and the action necessary.

2. Stage 2 of the Code represents a different matter. This is when the special educational needs co-ordinator takes the lead and he/she will wish to be advised of:

- the specific subject areas which continue to cause concern and how the relevant staff propose to provide the intensive help required.
- the needs of subject staff, in terms of teaching techniques, materials and

resources.

- the support arrangements to be made either within or outside of the classroom and their timetabling implications.
- implications of 'withdrawal teaching' and how lessons missed due to timetabling problems can be repeated.
- information relating to differentiation in the subject areas causing concern. At the very minimum, this means ensuring that the child is able to comprehend and deal effectively with the requirements of the curriculum, with a degree of success. Differentiation must not be confused with a dilution of the curriculum where a child is expected to do less or is only able to complete a task with help. Teachers should therefore ensure that differentiation is both by task and by outcome.
- the records to be kept, especially in subject areas of concern.

3. From Stage 2 onwards, the process of co-ordination assumes greater significance and if this is to proceed smoothly, the following will be necessary:
- a contact person or point of reference for all parties particularly for the child and his or her parents needs to be agreed fairly early on, normally the child's tutor at Stage 1 and the special educational needs co-ordinator from Stage 2 onwards, working closely with the year tutor;
- information needs to be channelled consistently through the above source, making sure this person has all the necessary information readily at hand to deal with any queries, requirements, proposals or recommendations.

4. Choosing options in Year 9 (i.e at 14 years of age) represents another critical stage which secondary teachers need to be especially aware of, both leading to and after the consultation meetings with parents. Parents and indeed children will expect to receive clear advice and guidance relating to their performance, fully documented and clearly explained to enable them to make informed decisions as to which options to select. Children at different stages of the Code of Practice will need this information, together with advice on how possible difficulties can be provided for when pursuing certain subjects, e.g. literacy requirements in History, maths in Geography, in addition to the requisite skills in some subjects, e.g. reasoning, and deduction, in Maths and Science, and perceptual, creative skills in Drama and Art. Strategies to bypass avoidable difficulties with access can also be discussed, e.g. the use of word processing with spell checks, voice activated dictaphones, taped texts, differentiated worksheets for a child with a specific literacy difficulty or braille resources for a child with visual impairment. Furthermore, supervision and safety requirements in some subjects will need addressing, e.g. safety in Science, Home Economics and P.E.

5. The preparation of Individual Education Plans is also likely to present different requirements in the secondary school. It will be left to the specialist, the subject teacher, to prepare this. The essential requirement is for learning to take place and to progress at a satisfactory pace. This requires:
- a clear appreciation of the skills, knowledge and understanding necessary at different stages of the child's development;
- a breakdown of these into manageable components, with clear teaching objectives and timescales for their achievement;
- a willingness to look beyond one's subject area, e.g. to make allowances

for the literacy components of maths worksheets, science;
- a willingness to work and collaborate with other subject teachers;
- a willingness to be flexible with teaching style, pace and lesson content.

6. Finally, the preparation of Transition Plans in Year 9 will require careful planning and co-ordination within and between subject departments. This replaces the statutory reassessment procedures which used to take place under the terms of the 1981 Education Act. As a requirement of the 1993 Education Act, the importance of ensuring a clear, comprehensive and coherent plan cannot be too strongly emphasised.

The Transition Plan is intended to prepare for the child's smooth transition from school, with arrangements made well beforehand to ensure that his future needs and requirements are effectively met. The LEA takes the lead in the preparation of Transition Plans at meetings which run in tandem with Year 9 Annual Reviews. However, it is the responsibility of schools to supply the information to be included in the Plan.

Transition Plan – key issues

The key issues regarding preparation of the Transition Plan are:

1. *The child's educational and vocational requirements at post 16 years of age*
This will require information about the curriculum needed – that is, whether or not a full mainstream curriculum is envisaged. The child might be able to follow A level studies or might be better suited for an NVQ course. This would need to be established, including any special requirements to ensure full access to the course – for example, a child without use of the upper limbs who undertakes chemistry or computer studies at A level, or a wheelchair bound child wishing to attend a college without lifts or facilities for the disabled. Some children might prefer and be more suited to a vocational course, e.g. children with moderate learning difficulties or with basic skills deficits. In these cases, courses and their support requirements will need to be identified early; i.e. any special component with which the child might require help, e.g. simple maths for estimation, timekeeping and budgeting.

2. *Staffing and supervision arrangements*
Staffing and training needs should be addressed prior to pupil admission. If specialists are required to continue their involvement, e.g. physiotherapists, audiologists, teachers of the visually impaired, occupational therapists, they would need to be alerted and involved at and beyond the Transition Plan stage. Their advice may also be needed by the post 16 establishment on matters such as the siting and number of ramps, disabled toilets and lifts.

3. *Review arrangements, following preparation of Transition Plan*
On completion of the Transition Plan, there will be some two years before the child transfers to the next stage of his education. Therefore, the Plan will require review and updating yearly and this will be the responsibility of the secondary school staff, probably the special educational needs co-ordinator, assisted by the relevant teaching and non-teaching staff.

Conclusion

It often appears that when the child transfers from primary to secondary schooling, the focus changes from teaching the child to teaching the subject. This should not be the case. The emphasis should always be to teach the child; only in this way can the detailed knowledge about his needs translate into effective teaching objectives to ensure progress with the curriculum. It is, however, recognised that the performance of secondary schoolteachers is likely to be measured on their pupils' attainments in public examinations. Indeed, the introduction of market forces into education through the encouragement of competition between schools, open enrolment, parental choice and the publication of league tables, almost makes this a necessity (Potts, Armstrong and Masterton, 1995).

The culture of the market place requires the identification and evaluation of performance indicators which currently emphasise examination attainments. However, other factors are also important such as the school ethos, its reputation for the good conduct and discipline of its pupils and its arrangements for children with special educational needs (see Ainscow, 1991; Skrtic, 1991).

CHAPTER 3

Implications for schools and governing bodies

Introduction

The Code makes some specific requirements of schools. In addition to the stages to be followed in the identification, assessment and provision for children with special educational needs, schools are expected to provide information about:

● their Special Educational Needs Policy, which should detail the particular arrangements which apply relating to the teaching and support of children with special educational needs;
● the 'responsible person' for special needs, who could be the headteacher, special needs Governor or special educational needs co-ordinator;
● the success or otherwise of the special educational needs arrangements, this being a requirement in Governors' reports to parents from August 1995.

Duties and responsibilities of governing bodies

The governing bodies of schools have 'to have regard to the Code'. This implies a clear responsibility to ensure that their thinking, planning and approach to special educational needs reflects best practice as suggested in the Code. There is, however, no immediate expectation that the Code's requirements will be fully integrated into schools' special educational needs policies, there being no specific time frames for this. Schools are being given time to develop their approaches and policies and whilst it is acknowledged that their starting points will differ, depending on their degree of readiness and previous record with regard to special educational needs, it is a requirement that the Code will be assimilated in their practice in the not too distant future.

Essentially, the role of the governing body will be to influence and support whole school policies and, in particular, to:

● formalise and produce the Special Educational Needs Policy;

- monitor, support and evaluate implementation of this Policy;
- report on its effectiveness to parents in the Governors' annual reports, including any significant changes made to it;
- include a summary of the Policy in school prospectuses for 1995/96 and thereafter;
- identify and name a 'responsible person', whose responsibility will be to be kept informed of children with special educational needs and to pass on this information to other parties who have a role in teaching and supporting the child;
- identify, make and report on provision made for children with special educational needs;
- ensure provision for the effective integration of children with special educational needs;
- identify gaps in provision and either;
  - remediate these, or
  - collaborate with other schools and governing bodies, or with the LEA, in order to rectify this, especially when it would be uneconomic for a particular school to respond on its own, e.g. providing expensive equipment, adjustments, adaptations for a 'rare' type of need, when it would make more sense to provide collectively for such special provision;
- ensure that a register is maintained for children with special educational needs; a possible format is provided in Appendix 1.

It is highly likely that governing bodies would wish to take the lead strategic role with regard to policy making and leave the operational issues and day to day implementation requirements to named members of staff. In practice, this could well mean that policy will be formulated by the governing body, in consultation with the headteacher and special educational needs co-ordinator (SENCO). The headteacher will then undertake responsibility for its management and implementation and will delegate its day to day operation to the co-ordinator, or in larger schools, to the special needs team. Figure 3.1. shows a possible scenario.

The School's Special Educational Needs Policy

The information to be included in special educational needs policies is now prescribed by Regulations (Special Educational Needs: Information, Regulations, Regulation 2 and Schedule 1). The main requirements are:
1. *Information about the special education provision available, and in particular*
- the school's objectives for special educational needs, including details of its admission policy;
- the name of the special educational needs co-ordinator and details of any specialist provision, e.g. specialism amongst the staff, special facilities, units;
- information about access for children with disabilities, e.g. adaptations to buildings, lifts, disabled toilets, technological aids.
2. *Information about the policies for identification, assessment and provision for children with special educational needs, and in particular*
- how resources are allocated to and amongst pupils with special educational needs, e.g. whether allocated to individuals or groups, funds from within school resources, top up by the LEA, names and number of support staff, means and

Children with special educational needs: hierarchies and responsibilities

STRATEGY/
POLICY
MAKING

MANAGEMENT

OPERATION

GOVERNING BODY

1. Agrees policy (and budget), bearing in mind need to have regard to the Code

2. Delegates responsibility for implementation of SEN Policy to 'Responsible Person', either:
    Governor for Special Educational Needs
    or
    Headteacher

HEADTEACHER

1. Oversees and reports on implementation of SEN Policy

2. Delegates responsibility for satisfactory operation to SENCO

SEN CO-ORDINATOR

1. Manages day to day operation of policy and reports to headteacher

2. Supports class teachers as and when required

3. Compiles and maintains SEN Register

4. Ensures Stages of the Code are followed and checks that the required documentation is kept and the appropriate action taken

5. Ensures IEPs are drawn up

6. Maintains contact with parents and support services

Figure 3.1 Special Educational Needs Policy: Strategy and Operation

frequency of support;

- the arrangements for assessing and reviewing pupils' needs, e.g. IEPs, use of assessments within the framework of the National Curriculum, teachers' observational assessments, record keeping, review procedures for IEPs, Annual Reviews;
- arrangements for facilitating access to a broad and balanced curriculum, including the National Curriculum, e.g. differentiation, use of technology for visually impaired children, provision of laptops, dictaphones, use of multi-sensory approaches to teaching, fieldwork facilities;
- approaches to integration, e.g. inclusion in all classes with support, aims and objectives of integration schemes, community involvement;
- criteria for evaluating success of the Special Educational Needs Policy, e.g. evidence of improved performance in specified areas, including academic and skills attainments, personal independence, social behaviour, study skills; the contribution and participation of staff and of parents; the whole school ethos, specialism/success with supporting children with special educational needs;
- complaints procedure, e.g. to whom, how, and the process in which the matter is to be dealt with and resolved, including timescales.

3. *Information about the school's staffing policies and partnership with outside agencies, including*

- policy on special educational needs training, e.g. in-house, bought in, external courses;
- support available from outside agencies, e.g. specialist staff from other schools, the LEA, the Health and Social Services;
- arrangements for partnership with parents, e.g. parents' evenings, Open Door policies, facilities for parents, appointment systems and response times, communication between home and school, home visiting; regularity, intensity and degree of informality in dealings with parents;
- links with other schools, colleges, employers.

Special educational needs policies are expected to provide the framework for schools to use in providing for children with special educational needs. They are intended to be developed by the whole staff, with leadership and support from individuals with the relevant expertise. This is to enable an effective, holistic and cross-curricular approach which focuses on differentiation and provision for the child as the integrating themes. The practicalities of implementation and the support systems and review mechanisms necessary can also be facilitated in this way, leading to a shared approach, agreed and understood by all parties, and therefore not seen to be the sole responsibility of the special educational needs co-ordinator.

The Regulations give policies a quasi-legal status but the active involvement of the governing body, together with the school's senior management, will be of the essence if a policy is to exceed the minimum legal requirements and become a live document for the whole staff to integrate in their practice.

The role of the special educational needs Governor

Special Educational Needs Governors frequently complain about lack of clarity or specificity with regard to their role. This was one of the findings from a survey carried out by the Advisory Centre for Education (ACE) in 1992/93. Other findings related to the lack of support likely to be available from either the Department for Education (DFE) or from LEAs in the discharge of their statutory duties.

It is crucial that governing bodies are clear from the start as to what is to be reasonably expected of their special educational needs governor. He or she will need a clear remit detailing the nature and extent of their responsibilities, amongst the most important of which are:

● the need to be fully conversant with legislation on the education of children with special educational needs. The legislation goes well beyond the Code of Practice and includes the 1993 Education Act, the 1989 Children Act and the 1988 Education Reform Act.

● the requirement to be aware of and to monitor the school's arrangements with regard to the identification, assessment and provision for children with special educational needs. This implies a familiarity with these arrangements through firsthand observation and experience, including close consultation with key members of school staff and parents.

● to represent and act as advocate on behalf of the child at meetings with external agencies, including those with the governing body. This means being fully informed about the child, funding and other school arrangements, and the requirements of staff and governors in respect of training and related special educational needs issues.

● to act as the main link for parents and others to the governing body. This includes convening and chairing working parties, influencing the School Development Plan and reporting regularly to governors.

It is important to note that these responsibilities require the governor to be a person of suitable experience and ability, able to inspire confidence beyond the governing body. The Advisory Centre for Education (ACE) suggests that this person should not be a 'novice appointment'; nor necessarily a governor with a 'particular personal concern about special needs'.

The role of the Special Educational Needs Co-ordinator

The Code allocates a key responsibility to the Special Educational Needs Co-ordinator (SENCO) and breaks new ground by requiring that there should be such a post in every school, with a named person to carry out the role and fulfil the responsibilities, which are to:

● ensure and facilitate the day to day implementation of the school's policy;
● liaise with, advise and support fellow teachers, and contribute to special educational needs training;
● liaise with parents and others, including support agencies;
● maintain the school's register for children with special educational needs, monitor and oversee records, e.g. IEPs, Annual Review documentation;
● co-ordinate provision for children with special educational needs.

The intention is that the co-ordinator acts as a consultant and a resource to fellow teachers. It should not be assumed that SENCO's will accept responsibility for the children because of the specific nature and title of their post. That responsibility rests with the class or subject teacher, who has the duty to make the provision as planned either in IEPs, the Statement or Annual Review targets and objectives. There are obviously implications for class teachers and co-ordinators in terms of time, planning, the availability of learning material and support staff. However, it is not thought that the Code's requirements will depart from existing good practice in schools.

How to formulate and write a Special Educational Needs Policy

1. Agree school's mission statement or equivalent at governors' meeting.
2. Use the mission statement to frame the Special Educational Needs Policy.
3. Define special needs policy in the context of:
   - the school's ethos
   - the school's needs and objectives
   - the school's aspirations for all children
   - the governing body's values and principles
   - the children's entitlement
   - parents' rights and expectations.
4. Detail in priority order:
   - the principal objectives of the Special Educational Needs Policy
   - the arrangements to operate within school to support the Policy and in particular, the financial and human resource arrangements.
5. Provide the names of key staff, including that of the Special Educational Needs Co-ordinator and of the Responsible Person, who are to act as links with parents and outside agencies.
6. Describe how:
   - children's learning difficulties are to be identified
   - children are to be helped
   - children's progress is to be reviewed and evaluated.
7. Include information relating to:
   - any specialism available from school staff
   - expertise that can be called or bought in
   - special facilities, resources
   - means of enabling access to these facilities.
8. Include details of the procedures and processes to be followed in the event of:
   - a query
   - a complaint.
9. Describe the consultation and partnership arrangements with:
   - parents and other parties
   - statutory agencies.
10. Include information on how success in achieving the objectives of the Policy is to be evaluated as well as its form and frequency of reporting.
11. Include a summary of the Policy in the school prospectus.

A photocopiable copy of the above is included as a checklist in Appendix 2.

A Schools' Charter for Parents and Children?

The current trend is for most services to produce a charter for their service users. This includes education and, in many ways, the Code of Practice can be interpreted to be a charter for children and parents in terms of their expectations and entitlements with regard to services, e.g. IEPs, time limits for statutory assessments and Special Educational Needs Tribunals for complaints. Governing bodies may wish to consider producing a charter for their schools. With regard to children with special educational needs, this should be a summary of the key issues from the Special Educational Needs Policy, described in no more than two to three pages and detailing:

- the service offered;
- the expectations that can be reasonably expected;
- the recourse available in the event of dissatisfaction or complaint.

Conclusion

It is crucial that schools are able to produce a balanced and informative Special Educational Needs Policy for circulation to parents. This is the basis of a contract against which the school's intentions, plans and efforts can be evaluated in terms of achievements, shortcomings and outcomes. The Policy, once publicised, is available for use by governors, parents, LEA staff and others to help their understanding of how the school intends to operate in supporting the children. From this information will be derived a variety of assumptions and expectations; so, the more precisely the policy is written, the less room there will be for confusion.

It is, therefore, suggested that the Policy should be written in a concise, factual manner, preferably with headings and in a style that is clear, jargon free and easily understandable to parents and others.

CHAPTER 4

Individual Education Plans

Introduction

Individual Education Plans (IEPs) represent one of the new requirements of the Code. They have a number of special features, and require the provision of particular information. They replace similar documentation used in the past and are intended to be 'live' documents, to be used in planning, implementation and review of learning programmes. Their format will vary from one authority to another and indeed from school to school. However, the essential requirements are that the IEP should:

Planning

- specify as clearly as possible the nature and extent of the child's learning difficulty;
- describe the action to be taken, the intervention programme to be implemented and the special educational provision to be made;

Action

- detail and allocate the staff to be involved and the frequency of support to be made available;
- specify the learning programmes and activities to be undertaken and the materials and equipment required;
- set specific targets to be achieved in a given time;
- include success criteria for the purpose of monitoring and evaluation;
- involve and empower parents, offering help wherever necessary;
- ascertain the child's views, wishes and perceptions and involve him in the implementation of his IEP;
- detail any pastoral care or medical requirements and ensure these are provided by the relevant agencies;

Review

- specify monitoring, assessment and review arrangements;
- include dates for formal reviews of the IEPs with parents involved;
- reviews can lead either to a higher or lower Stage within the staged assessments, e.g. if a child has made significant progress, he may be kept at the same stage (i.e. Stage 1, 2 or 3) for at least two reviews, at the end of which he may be reverted to an earlier stage or removed from the special educational

needs register. Conversely, he may need to be moved up a stage after the same review period if he fails to make the necessary progress.

The functions of the IEP are shown in the left hand side boxes. These serve to illustrate the planning, action and review functions that the IEP is intended to serve. These should feature centrally in all IEPs, the most useful ones of which will contain information relating to the targets being set, the success criteria to be used and the outcome achieved, together with details as to the monitoring, staffing and review arrangements.

Features of a good IEP

A good IEP will:
- identify the child's current attainments
- target specific, priority areas of difficulty
- show systematic use of diagnostic and assessment techniques in identifying and making provision for a learning difficulty.

Targets
- set targets which are:
  - directly related to the areas of the learning difficulty
  - specific, measurable, achievable, relevant and teachable within the timescale set for review and in relation to the teacher's knowledge about the pupil.

Success Criteria
- relate success criteria directly to targets, ensuring these can be objectively assessed and based on the teacher's knowledge of what can be expected from the child within the timescale specified
- specify indicators relating to success, e.g. frequency of behaviour/skill being taught, degree/frequency of fluency /accuracy achieved (e.g. in reading/spelling), rate of learning/speed at which skill is acquired.

Outcome
- include outcome measures which can be used to check if targets were:
  - realistic and achievable
  - moving on to the next step of attainment within the priority area.

Provision
- relate provision arrangements to the targets set and specify length and frequency of support.

Monitoring
- include record keeping arrangements and frequency/nature of liaison in the monitoring section.

Guidelines for completing an IEP

An Individual Education Plan is meant to be a working document which specifies precisely the action to be taken in order to meet a set of learning objectives. This requires a clear appraisal of the child's learning difficulties, followed by the setting of realistic, achievable teaching objectives, together with an indication of the resources, material and other facilities that will be required. These are the three essential elements of the IEP which can then be subjected to evaluation and review, within a continuous and systematic planning, teaching and review cycle.

In drawing up an IEP, it is tempting to try and address all of the child's difficulties and attempt to find a solution to all of them. This is a pointless exercise, and best avoided. Instead, teachers should:
- identify one or two areas of difficulty which they consider to be the priority for action;
- analyse the area(s) of difficulty leading to:
    - a clear picture as to the nature of the learning difficulty
    - a breakdown of the skills and sub-skills which the child requires to compensate for or overcome the learning difficulty
    - include a baseline as to what the child can and cannot do, for the purpose of monitoring and evaluation of the teaching programme;
- plan a teaching programme that focuses directly on the needs identified, keeping this specific to the identified priority area;
- set teaching objectives, taking account of the time frame being worked to; this implies a manageable number of short term objectives which can be used to demonstrate the progress achieved;
- specify their proposals in terms of teaching, counselling or other forms of support needed, e.g. from an assistant;
- specify the material to be used, how this is to be differentiated, the frequency of its use and, applicability to other areas of the curriculum;
- determine how the skill being taught will be consolidated, applied and transferred to all relevant areas;
- include success criteria and outcome measures in order to enable feedback and evaluation of the teaching programmes implemented.

Teachers might find the following guidelines helpful when preparing an IEP.
- prepare an IEP for a specific area of learning difficulty, i.e. do not attempt to address the issues of reading, behaviour or other difficulties all at once.
- beware of falling into the trap of selecting a generalised difficulty as the priority area of focus.
- if there is evidence of a difficulty that affects all areas of learning, e.g. lack of motivation, distractibility, or lack of application to school work, try to identify the root causes and see if these can be broken down into manageable tasks for remediation. For example, or lack of motivation could be the direct result of failure to achieve in learning, perhaps due to a lack of reading skills making the curriculum inaccessible. The child then develops this as a coping strategy to maintain self-esteem and the key task for the teacher is to address the development of literacy as the priority.

It is assumed that an IEP will have a section on:
- the nature of the difficulty;
- the action to be taken;
- the support arrangements;
- the arrangements for review;

Each will now be discussed in turn, with suggested guidelines on their completion.

The nature of the difficulty

There is no need to write at great length when completing this section. Bullet points can be used, as shown below for a child who has literacy difficulties and for whom an IEP is being drawn up. This focuses on remediation of his reading difficulties. The focus is on reading only, though the child is known to have other problems. Listing too many of these makes the IEP process unmanageable.

- *John aged 8, has a sight vocabulary of ten words, as assessed on a 100 key word list.*
- *He recognises letter sounds, with the exception of vowels.*
- *He has a reading age of below six years, as assessed on the British Ability Scales word Reading Test.*

If possible, include within this section information about what the child can do. This helps with planning. The example concerning John, shows some of the tasks possible, e.g. teaching of vowel sounds, increase in sight vocabulary, curriculum implications for an eight year old who is not reading at the level required.

The action to be taken

Teaching targets Include in this section the teaching targets. These should be short term so that they may be reviewed within the IEP period. For John, the teaching targets might be:

- increase sight vocabulary to 15 words within six weeks and to 20 words within the school term;
- teach vowel sounds and ensure mastery within a term;
- provide material that has been differentiated, taking account of John's low reading ability;
- enable John to have access to reading material at his interest level, by reading to him for a short period every day from a book of his choice.

Material, resources, approaches to be used Include here any special material the child will require. Books on tape, use of language master cards, word books, all come to mind for a child with a reading difficulty. Approaches, on the other hand, might include the development of phonics or word attack skills or the use of multi-sensory approaches to reading. If the approach is well known there should not be a requirement for a great deal of detail here, as further information can be found from other sources.

Success criteria Teachers sometimes find it confusing to differentiate between a teaching target and success criteria. Essentially, the teaching target represents the goal set by the teacher, i.e. what the teacher intends to achieve. Success criteria, on the other hand, provide the measure which the teacher decides will be acceptable at various stages in aiming for the complete achievement of the teaching targets. They help to show the extent to which the targets are being achieved and for what proportion of the time. For example, if the target is to increase sight vocabulary to 20 words within 12 weeks, the success criteria might be:

- recognition of 12 key words, 50 per cent of the time after Week 1, 75 per cent of the time after Week 2, to recognition of 20 key words 100 per cent of the time within 12 weeks. This will represent complete achievement of the teaching target and the success criteria will reflect this, or not, as the case may be, e.g. if recognition of the key words was only achieved 50 per cent of the time.

It should be clear, therefore, that the success criteria refer to performance which is considered acceptable at different phases of the teaching programme. They represent the milestones and help to break the tasks into simpler and smaller steps, providing a measure of the success being achieved. They are a helpful tool for planning and though they represent the teacher's estimate of what to expect and their assumption of the child's rate of learning, they can be easily modified in the light of teaching and experience.

Outcomes Include here the actual outcomes or results of the learning programmes. How do these compare with the teaching targets set and the success criteria selected? Were these outcomes as expected? Did they exceed expectations, or were they disappointing?

The support arrangements Specify in this section who does what, when, how long for and how often? Also include the supervision and monitoring arrangements if teaching is being delegated to another member of staff, especially if this is a special needs assistant (SNA). It would be wrong to expect a special needs assistant to deal with a complex learning difficulty on their own and the teacher needs to remember that this does not absolve teachers from their responsibility. Times for planning, meetings, or other purposes such as co-ordinating programmes where a number of people are involved, also require inclusion.

The arrangements for review

It goes without saying that any teaching should be the subject of continuous monitoring and review. However, include here the times and dates for formal planning and reviews between all parties. It might be helpful to differentiate between in-school planning, restricting this to school staff only, and the wider meeting open to parents. The former can take place more frequently and informally, with the focus on planning, intervention and co-ordination. The latter can then serve to inform and involve parents on what has been achieved and what is outstanding.

Problem Analysis

A Selection of Strategies and Approaches

SWOT analysis

In preparing IEPs, a useful approach to adopt is that commonly known as SWOT analysis (see fig 4.1), from which a plan can be derived. SWOT is shorthand for *Strengths, Weaknesses, Opportunities* and *Threats*. The first two represent the internal processes or characteristics of the problem – those pertaining to the child, e.g. what he or she can and cannot do. The latter are more to do with external or outside forces, e.g. what the problem represents to a third party, the teaching opportunities and threats faced by the teacher who is trying to help a child with a learning difficulty.

SWOT analysis is a useful discipline at the stage of describing the nature of the child's learning difficulty. The *strengths* when identified provide the starting points, the baseline which can be used later to evaluate progress. The *weaknesses* help with the setting of teaching targets. The *opportunities* help focus the teacher's mind on the range of possibilities to try and the *threats* (and obstacles) likely to be encountered and to be dealt with.

This case study is an example of a SWOT analysis.

Case Study

Rob is a pleasant, sociable and co-operative 15 year old who was born with congenital abnormalities in his limbs. His upper limbs are only five inches long and he has no hand or fingers, the arms stopping at the elbow. His lower limbs are also short and both end at the knee. He is fitted with prosthetic aids which enable him to be fully mobile so that he can participate fully in most physical activities. He uses his chin and his mouth to handle P.E. and sports equipment such as a tennis racket. He uses a pencil in his mouth to operate computer equipment and is learning the use of a dictaphone to dictate his work.

Rob attends a mainstream secondary school where he has the support of a part-time special needs assistant. He is making very good progress with his learning and is expected to do well in Computer Studies, English, Maths, Science, Geography, Religious Studies, Drama and French in his GCSE examinations. His main problems are, as expected, in practical activities which require fine motor co-ordination and these are when he requires the help of his special needs assistant.

Rob has the support of devoted and supportive parents. They are pleased that he is doing so well but are concerned about the future, believing that he will always require additional support as he will be unable to be completely independent.

Rob accepts that there are limitations to the range of opportunities likely to be available to him in the future. However, he is determined to use his strengths in computing to work towards a career in information technology though he is worried that he may not be able to engage in the engineering and repair aspects of working with computers.

SWOT analysis: interpretation and discussion

The SWOT analysis (see fig 4.1) clearly shows the areas where useful work can be carried out, taking account of the child's strengths and weaknesses. It also helps identify the opportunities for the teacher to use the resources of the child, the parents and other agencies, including LEA support staff. The constraints are also clear: a tight financial budget, the range of realistic possibilities and options for Rob and his need for support due to his inability to be completely independent.

A SWOT analysis helps to focus on the main issues to be addressed in planning and intervention. It enables the teacher to be aware of both the internal and external constraints in planning relating to:

- the teacher himself or herself;
- the child;
- the key players with a stake in the child's education, e.g. parents, headteacher, governors and LEA staff;
- environmental constraints, e.g. class size, peer group, community attitudes, school ethos;

SWOT Analysis	
Strengths	*Weaknesses*
Personality	*Physical disability*
Sociable, co-operative, responsive.	Absence of limbs is a severe handicap, not sufficiently compensated by prosthetic aids. Fine motor tasks cause Rob significant problems.
Determination	*Dependence*
Clear willingness to participate in activities, including those where a physical disability would be a severe handicap.	Rob needs help with some practical activities, especially where safety is a prime consideration.
Ability	*Stamina*
At least average intelligence and able to deal effectively with requirements of mainstream curriculum. Predicted to achieve good grades in GCSE exams.	Rob tires easily and has to put in considerably more effort in his physical activities.
Opportunities	*Threats*
Willing child, supportive parents. Supportive management and Governors.	No clear prognosis about the future. Extent of risk taking possible: What if anything were to go wrong? Tight financial budget.
Level of co-operation	*Lack of expertise*
Rob has the will to succeed and is prepared to co-operate with teaching arrangements. Active co-operation of LEA staff.	Rob is the only severely disabled child the school has had to provide for. Teachers heavily dependent on other experts.
Use of strengths	*Disability*
Rob has many strengths which could be usefully used to compensate for his physical disability. His communication and cognitive skills can be exploited to the full.	Absence of Rob's limbs makes planning the curriculum difficult. This partially succeeds because of his determination.
The future	*The future*
Rob has a clear vision about the future. This facilitates direction setting, choice of options and decision making, taken in consultation with him.	Rob's aspirations present a challenge. Should be restricted to only those areas in which he is currently succeeding.

Figure 4.1: SWOT Analysis of a child with a physical disability

- financial and human resource implications, e.g. budgetary situation, availability of support staff, level of expertise;
- range and adequacy of learning material available.

All of the above are relevant to Rob's education and can be applied in turn to determine the action needed to ensure his continuing, successful integration in the mainstream. Rob represents an excellent example of how a child with apparently the most severe and disabling condition can succeed in the mainstream.

PEST analysis

It is usual to combine a SWOT analysis with a PEST analysis. This enables analysis of the wider external environment from a number of perspectives to supplement the SWOT findings which essentially relate to the child himself.

PEST is shorthand for analysis of the *Political, Economic, Sociological* and *Technological* environment. This is normally done at the macro-level, which means looking at issues within the national context – government, politics and attitude, education budgets, values and developments in education, information technology and the use of computers in schools including other technological advances.

PEST analysis ensures an awareness of global issues. It helps focus on the wider context of how external forces dictate on what goes on in the classroom. Teachers may, therefore, wish to think about these issues when preparing their strategies. A modified approach, particularly useful for their purpose would be to conduct a PEST analysis as it relates to their own circumstances, e.g. their school/LEA, the political structure, practices and attitudes of County Councillors, Governors; budgetary health of their LEA/schools; the community they serve, the support and involvement of parents; the technological resources and expertise available within their school/LEA.

Force field analysis

Once the SWOT analysis is completed, teachers might be interested to carry out a further analysis to identify the forces for and against change in respect of either the child or the environment they are working in. This is known in the literature as 'Force field analysis' (see Carnall, 1989, for details). It basically represents an attempt to identify the factors pushing for and against change in both the child's internal and external environment. The Force field diagram (Figure 4.2) shows the forces for and against change for a child with a behaviour problem in a secondary school.

Conclusion

It is often the case, as examples in this chapter show that a child has a combination of difficulties in learning, including physical, language, emotional, behavioural problems. In these instances, it is advisable to try and deal with each problem one at a time and, if need be, draw up more than one IEP. This is required as the targets, support arrangements, material and resources are likely to be different, making it cumbersome to include all the information in one document. By using separate documentation for each area, it is easier to plan the workload, ascertain the potential for success with the tasks set and monitor action and progress. The main problem would be with co-ordination, to avoid duplication or non-attention to the peripheral, overlap areas. However, it should be remembered that the intention of the IEP is to concentrate on the priority problem and to ensure that the focus leads to identifiable results, hence the need to be selective and specific if this focussed, concentrated approach is to be maintained.

The remaining pages of this chapter contain specimen Individual Education Plans (Specimens A, B and C). Examples of other formats of IEPs are included in Appendix 3.

Forces for change	Forces for change
Teacher Need for control in class In the interests of the other children In teacher's own interest	*Child* Wish to improve behaviour Wish to be accepted and seen to be the same as the other children Wish to make progress and waste less time on unproductive behaviours
Expectations of significant others Change required by – headteacher – governing body – parent	*Expectations of significant others* Will not be tolerated for much longer Threat of exclusion Disapproval
Forces against change	Forces against change
Teacher Too difficult/time consuming to deal with problem Easier to ask for child to be removed from class Exclusion may be a preferable option long term No resources for this child; demands beyond the teacher/school Child does not fit in with school culture/priorities	*Child* Behaviour leads to attention and status Behaviour is legitimate to deal with perceived injustice Exclusion is one way out of the unbearable situation of school No real expectation of being able to change. School culture alien to child's perceived needs/priorities

Figure 4.2: Force field diagram to show forces for and against change in respect of a child with emotional and behavioural difficulties

Individual Education Plan (Specimen A)

Name: David S   **Date of Birth:** 12.11.86   **School:** XYZ   **Teacher:** Karen D

Strengths and Weaknesses   Priority: Spelling and Writing

Strengths	Weaknesses
David can: • Read at the level of an eight and half year old • Read the books and worksheets used in class • Concentrate for a minimum of 5 minutes and up to 10 minutes • Co-operate and work effectively with his peers	David cannot: • Write legibly • Spell 90 per cent of words he tries to include in his writing (he has a spelling age of 6 years as assessed on the Vernon Graded Spelling Test) • Undertake written work without support/encouragement and does not complete written assignments

Teaching Objectives (derived from 1 above)

Objectives	Strategy
David will: • Increase his spelling vocabulary by 5 words a week • Copywrite one piece of work for 5 minutes daily and must produce at least two lines of legible writing in his book • Complete one written assignment, estimated to require 10 minutes in Week 1, increasing to 12 minutes in Week 2, 14 minutes in Week 3 and increasing to 28 minutes by Week 10	David is to: • Learn one word a day from list given by class teacher. This will be checked three times a day, twice at school and once at home *Action:* Class teacher to devise teaching approach and to agree strategy with Mrs S • Be shown exactly the standard required and given regular feedback *Action:* Class teacher • Be supervised and supported in his efforts by the Special Needs Assistant and will have his work checked by the teacher, on completion
Success Criteria • Gains in spelling vocabulary by 5 words a week, David being successful at spelling new words learned 50 per cent of the time on first check, 100 per cent of the time on second check and 100 per cent of the time on third check • Increase in spelling age by 6 to 9 months in school year	**Contingency Arrangements** • Review targets set, in the light of David's performance • Adjust level of supervision/support to match • Review/Revise teaching method/strategy and consult with Special Educational Needs Co-ordinator and/or other colleague if necessary

Provision	Monitoring Arrangements
Materials and resources • School's teaching package on spelling • Books used in class • Language master cards for David to use so that he can check spelling on his own Staffing • Special Needs Assistant time • Class teacher time (these can be quantified)	• Daily checks and written records for information of all parties • Weekly planning and review meetings between class teacher and Special Needs Assistant, to include Special Educational Needs Co-ordinator when necessary • Weekly communication with Mrs S through note in home/school book • Meeting with Mrs S twice a term

Outcome	
(Record outcome here)	(Date completed):

Individual Education Plan (Specimen B)

Name: John S   Date of Birth: 23.6.86   Date completed: 10.9.94.

Nature of Learning Difficulty: Weaknesses in literacy + emotional difficulties
Priority for action: To implement programme for literacy

John has been experiencing problems with his reading and spelling since he joined FL school in September 1994. He has:
- difficulty decoding words and has a sight vocabulary of approximately 10 words (as assessed on list of 100 key words)
- a reading age of 6 years at chronological age 8 years 6 months, placing him at the second centile
- a spelling age of under 6 years, failing to score on the Vernon Graded Word Spelling Test (below the second centile).

He reads very slowly and tends to memorise texts, often making wild guesses. His handwriting is untidy and ill formed. He is able to produce very little work without support: usually two lines of illegible material in 40 minute sessions.

Date of meeting	Present	Action notes
9.9.94	AB, CD, EF, Mrs S	1. Implement literacy programme prepared by Special Educational Needs Co-ordinator, teacher adviser and class teacher, as agreed with Mrs S

Targets	Success Criteria	Outcome
1. Increase sight vocabulary	1. Sight vocabulary of 15 words, by December 1994	
2. Enable John to read, through the use of decoding and phonic skills	2. Read one page from his story book, by November 1994	
3. Improve handwriting skills through cursive script	3. Writing is joined up, with spacing and 40 per cent of John's work is legible	

Provision

1. Multi-sensory programme as advised by Specialist Teacher Adviser (STA), using school's reading schemes
1.1. Implementation

Reading
- John is helped with his reading for 15 minutes, twice daily, on a one-to-one basis with Special Needs Assistant (SNA)
- John spends 15 minutes with class teacher in a group of five working on a literacy task
- shared reading at home with his mother for 20 minutes each day

Spelling
- ten minutes each day on Hampshire Special Needs Spelling, with SNA on a one-to-one basis and in small groups
- ten minutes, on his own, working with Talking Pendown
- two words a day to be learned at school, checked at home and rechecked the next day at school; build up to 10 a week (mainly high frequency words)

Handwriting
- ten minutes each day on handwriting practice, copying out list of spelling words learned, with addition of new ones

Monitoring arrangements

Home support
Weekly meetings between:
  SNA/class teacher to plan work,
  check on progress and update
  records

Daily briefing of SNA by teacher, plus informal contact
Monthly review with Special Educational Needs Co-ordinator/STA

Weekly communication with his mother via home-school book and termly meetings of approximately 30 minutes at school

Individual Education Plan (Specimen C)

(If behaviour was chosen as a priority, then the following IEP could have been prepared)

Nature of difficulty and priority for action: Behaviour

2. John's behaviour has been deteriorating since around March 1994. This coincides with the break up of the family, his father leaving home and not making contact with him since. He says that he is deeply upset at this and that he is not able to concentrate on his work for longer than a couple of minutes because:

- his mind is on other matters as he worries about his mother's and family's welfare a great deal

- he is failing with his work, being unable to deal with the literacy requirements

- he is distracted by the other children

- he finds that he gets attention when he is 'playing the fool', wandering round the class, shouting out, tearing his work, answering back; this happens on average, once hourly

Targets	Success Criteria
1. Improve concentration and co-operative behaviour	1.1. Improved concentration to 5 minutes, for on task behaviour, and 7 minutes, for co-operative behaviour without distracting
	1.2. John works co-operatively with one other person for 5 minutes, by October 1994
	1.3. Tasks estimated to take 15 minutes completed by John within 20 minutes by December 1994
2. Increase periods of time without distracting	2.1. John stays seated for 10 minutes, by October 1994
	2.2. Calling out reduces to twice a day
3. Enable John to:	3.1. John spends 15 minutes daily with teacher and agrees plan for the day – achieves 50 per cent success
- talk about his worries, anxieties and anger	3.2. Use of soft chair as a strategy, reduces frequency of frustration displays by 50 per cent
- follow strategy of removing himself to the soft chair in the classroom to control his frustrations/anger and alert class teacher to his needs	3.3. John takes pride in his achievements and completes 50 per cent of the tasks he is allocated
- improve his self-esteem by being more positive about himself	

CHAPTER 5

Stages of the Code of Practice

The Code suggests a staged approach to the identification, assessment and provision in respect of children's special educational needs. Five stages are suggested, with Stage 1 being the earliest and Stage 5 representing the point at which special educational needs become the subject of statutory assessment. A number of elements are necessary at each stage and these are described below, with an indication of the processes involved, the responsibilities implied and the requirements to be met.

Stage 1: Initial concern: Introduction

This is the first stage when a learning difficulty is suspected or a concern registered, either from class teachers or from parents. This might have arisen from observation of the child's behaviour or learning, in the sense that normal expectations are not being met. For example, the child may be showing signs of difficulty in comprehending instructions in class, needing to refer back to the teacher for clarification, simplification or even at times for reassurance. Careful assessment and observation might reveal that he is able to respond appropriately to teacher tasks when instructions are given in small groups, on an individual basis or in calm, quiet environments. This might lead to suspicion of a hearing or listening difficulty, especially in young children, and this is when parents need to be contacted or medical notes studied to check on any history of a hearing difficulty. Speed would be of the essence here, if the child is to learn and progress normally.

   The point to note is that it is usually individuals with the most direct contact with the child who should notice if something is wrong. This includes other children, support staff, special needs assistants and dinner ladies. In this way, a complete picture of the child within and beyond the school day can be constructed and the basis of the difficulty identified. Questions which could be asked at this stage are:

1. What skills/behaviour should the child be showing at this stage of his development?

2. How far behind is this child compared to his peers? Is this a significant delay and why? Is this affecting relationships with peers?

3. Is the child's attitude and disposition for learning being affected? Does he seem to have problems with access to the curriculum? What can be done to help?

4. How do the parents feel about their child's development/progress? Can they shed any light on the problem?

5. Who is the best person to contact for help?

This list is not meant to be exhaustive but is intended to provide a structured approach towards reflecting upon and making sense of the child's problems. Most of the information should be available without too much effort and normally, at Stage 1, it will be assumed that the class or subject teacher would have done the groundwork and be in a position to formalise the response the child requires.

Stage 1: Summary

Stage 1 encompasses
- the initial identification of a learning difficulty;
- the gathering of information;
- recording and registration of the child's special educational needs, including the planning and teaching response;
- consultation with parents.

Processes
- the trigger for Stage 1 assessment is when a teacher, parent or other professional gives evidence of concern;
- Stage 2 is reached if, after two reviews at Stage 1, special help has not resulted in satisfactory progress: if on the other hand, the child has made sufficient progress, he need not stay on the SEN Register if the progress is maintained over a period of two reviews.

Responsibilities
- responsibility for assessing children, differentiating teaching and devising appropriate plans remains with the class or subject teacher;
- the class teacher must inform the headteacher, parents and SENCO who registers the child's special educational needs;
- the class teacher can ask for help from the SENCO, school doctor, or other professional agency;
- support services (educational psychologist, CMOs, specialist teachers) can be called in from Stage 1, and always at Stage 3.

Requirements
- the parents' and child's own views on the learning difficulties must be sought;
- any known health, pastoral or social problems are to be detailed, together with:
  - profiles of achievement
  - National Curriculum Attainments
  - other information from testing and other forms of assessment
  - record of school attendance;
- records must be kept of:

- the nature of the concern
- the action taken
- the targets set
- the time when progress is to be reviewed (normally within a term or six months, with parents kept informed).

Stage 2: Recognition of need for 'intensive' action

Stage 2 is reached after systematic and documented intervention over a period of time. The child's needs would normally have been dealt with at Stage 1 for at least two terms of the school year and positive action taken, in consultation with parents and with their involvement. The child's name would have been recorded on the school's SEN register and records, preferably an IEP, would be available to show the information gathered, the learning programmes or management strategies implemented, the reviews held with parents and the targets achieved. Normally, the child's progress will be monitored on a termly basis.

If progress is not forthcoming, this would imply that:
- the child has a persistent learning difficulty, requiring intensive teaching and support;
- the child's needs require more detailed assessment and advice, leading to the provision of regular and systematic help;
- the cycle of assessing, teaching and reviewing should be more systematically monitored, with more frequent evaluation of teaching and review with regard to the efficacy of the teaching approaches and arrangements, including the appropriateness of the learning material.

Questions to ask at Stage 2 are:

Learning difficulties

What is now known about the child's learning difficulty?
What methods have been tried and which ones have been more successful?
Are there any areas where practice could be improved?

Priority

What is the priority area for attention and remediation?
Does this need to be broken down into sub-areas so that manageable objectives can be set?

Teaching strategy

Why did the child not respond to the arrangements made at Stage 1?
Where are adjustments/revisions required?
Should the focus be more on the child's learning style or greater differentiation of the curriculum?
Should teaching be in even smaller steps?

Staffing arrangements

What staffing arrangements need to be made to provide the child with the intensive help that he needs?

How will this help be secured, organised, monitored and evaluated?

Most children should respond to the arrangements made at Stage 2, bearing in mind that they would have attracted a focused, systematic teaching approach to deal with their learning difficulty. Evaluation of their progress would normally be made at their IEP reviews and decisions on whether or not they need to move up or down a stage can normally be made following two consecutive reviews.

A photocopiable copy of this checklist is included in Appendix 4.

Stage 2: Summary

This encompasses the seeking and provision of further assessment and advice, including the creation of an Individual Education Plan, with a view to implementing *intensive* help.

Process

- the SENCO takes the lead in:
  - assessing the child's learning difficulty
  - planning a programme of intervention
  - monitoring and supporting its delivery
  - reviewing and evaluating the effectiveness of the teaching arrangements and provision made;
- the SENCO may seek additional information or advice from Health, Social Services or other agencies after consultation with parents, and agree appropriate action with them and with the child's teachers;
- review of Stage 2 should take place within a term and parents are to be invited;
- parents must be consulted if planning to move to Stage 3.

Requirements

- **an IEP to be drawn up;**
- **the IEP should set out:**
  - the nature of the child's learning difficulty
  - specific learning targets
  - the materials and resources to be used, including any special provision
  - the staff to be involved and the frequency of support to be made
  - the timescale within which work is to be carried out
  - monitoring and assessment arrangements
  - date for review.

Stage 3: Early intensive help with external support

Stage 3 applies to a small minority of children whose needs are so complex as to require even more help than the intensive arrangements provided at Stage 2. In terms of the 'Warnock 20 per cent', these children are likely to be functioning towards the bottom end of the range, towards the 2 per cent of children who have special educational needs. This does not mean that they will be in the bottom 2 per cent in all areas. Their educational profile should show strengths in some areas and weaknesses in the development of the skills calling for remediation, e.g. a fourteen year old who has achieved Level 7 of the

National Curriculum in Maths and Science but who is struggling with spelling and presentation of his work though able to deal with the reading components of the curriculum. Obviously, these difficulties would have been identified earlier and provided for at Stages 1 and 2. It is only when they prove to be persistent and resistant to teaching and remediation that Stage 3 processes would be called for. The implication clearly is that the previous stages would have demonstrated careful and systematic planning, collaboration between teachers and others and creativity on the teacher's part in trying a number of measures targeted at the area of concern. It is not necessary to wait for Stage 3 in order to use external specialist help and advice; this can and should be done at any time if considered useful. It is best to tackle a problem early than to wait.

At Stage 3, external agencies are routinely called in and they would wish to establish that:

• support has been made available to the child over a period of time and has been systematically and appropriately implemented. This is to ensure that the teaching programmes and other forms of intervention have indeed been exhausted. Sometimes they are not, and some adjustments may be needed.

• intervention has been based on comprehensive assessment, with documentation available to assist with further planning and evaluation. This is particularly important with regard to children who have emotional and behavioural difficulties. Such documentation should have a balanced focus. For example, it would be inappropriate to have detailed records of incidents relating to the child's unacceptable behaviour, without equivalent information on the steps and strategies taken to deal with the problem.

• the necessary information relating to a child's difficulty is available, e.g. medical information about a physical or sensory problem, even though these may be mild and easily overlooked. Mild clumsiness, loss of concentration and periods of inattention, lack of spontaneous response, twitching of muscles and restlessness in class, may all be significant but may not have been explored fully, with the school doctor for example. Similarly, home circumstances may not be well known to the teacher, e.g. parents' illnesses, domestic circumstances. Marriage break up may have a considerable effect on the child's learning and need to be taken into account when planning teaching programmes.

Teachers might wish to ask the following questions, if considering moving a child to Stage 3:

Nature of learning difficulty

Are the child's needs so complex as to require significantly more help and a different type of approach to that provided earlier?

Teaching and assessment

Have the teaching interventions been systematically planned and given sufficient time to work?
Have these been based on concrete evidence of assessment? Give details.
Which areas of the child's functioning seem to be more resistant to change?

Priorities for action and performance indicators

What are the priority areas to address?

What would serve as useful indicators to monitor and evaluate progress?

Consensus on learning difficulty

What is the consensus of opinion on the child's learning difficulty?
Does the child/parent/teacher/support staff feel that: (a) appropriate and (b) sufficient help has been given?

Consultation with teachers

Have all teachers been consulted? (It is essential in secondary schools to consult with teachers and establish their views. In which areas do they feel the child is doing well? Which strategies are more likely to bear fruit?)

Consultation with parents

How do parents feel about the whole process?
Do they believe that they have been adequately consulted/involved?

Consultation with the child

How does the child feel?
Does the child understand and is he committed to the plan?
Does the child consider it realistic and what level of responsibility is he prepared/able to accept?

Standards setting and contingency planning

Have expectations and standards been clearly specified? Give details.
Which support structures are required to facilitate achievement of these? What are they?
What are the contingency arrangements to deal with problems, failures and unplanned events?
 These questions are set out in the style of a usable form in Appendix 5.

Stage 3: Summary

The school calls on outside specialist help.
Process
• responsibility for pupils with special educational needs is shared between class teacher, SENCO and outside support teachers (such as educational psychologists);
• external agencies may offer:
 – classroom support
 – advice on teaching approaches, materials, technology or classroom management
 – direct teaching;
• review to be organised by the SENCO within a term to:
 – include and involve parents (and where possible the child)
 – focus on progress made
 – report on effectiveness of the IEP
 – update information in the light of progress made and make future plans;
• if progress is not satisfactory, the headteacher, in consultation with all parties involved may consider referring the child to the LEA for a statutory assessment.

- IEP to be completed, following consultation and advice from support services;
- the IEP should detail
  - teaching targets and strategies to be used
  - assessment undertaken, methods tried and known outcomes
  - teaching arrangements, building on experiences derived at Stage 2
  - monitoring, review and evaluation arrangements;
- following on from Stage 3, a range of documentation and evidence will be required to support a referral to the LEA for statutory assessment, should this be needed. This should
  - include educational and developmental profiles
  - summarise the views of the parents and of the child
  - itemise any health or social factor likely to have an influence on the child's learning
  - show evidence of strategies tried and the progress achieved
  - demonstrate a co-ordinated approach in the planning and teaching response, including the involvement of professionals with relevant knowledge and expertise outside the normal competence of the school
  - consistent and systematic delivery of the teaching and other approaches agreed, including effective use of any special resources targeted for the child
  - emphasise and demonstrate the effectiveness of the teaching input as opposed to searching for within-child factors to explain lack of progress
  - show evidence of a planned and co-ordinated intervention over time.

Stage 4: Considering the need for statutory assessment

Stage 4 represents the point at which stages cease to be wholly school based. This is when schools and the LEA have to co-operate and share responsibility in assessing and providing for children with special educational needs.

Stage 4 is reached if it is considered that the child's needs should be subject to the statutory assessment procedures laid down by the 1993 Education Act. It does not mean, however, that the assessment will necessarily lead to the production of a Statement of Special Educational Needs. This has caused much confusion in the past, not helped by the use of such terms as 'Statementing'. What essentially happens at Stage 4 is the collection of professional advice and evidence by the LEA to enable it to make a decision on whether or not to proceed with statutory assessment.

If the LEA decides to proceed, it will request advice and evidence from a range of professionals, including parents, doctors, teachers, social workers and educational psychologists as to how best to provide for a child with special educational needs. If, on the other hand, it decides that there is no basis to initiate a statutory assessment, it has to give reasons as to why not and, if the request for statutory assessment came directly from parents, must do so within a specified time limit. The time limit does not apply if the request originated from school.

Stage 4 therefore represents a process which ensues when a child is referred to the LEA for statutory assessment. It goes without saying that the responsibilities identified at previous stages would be ongoing and would require to be met, irrespective of the LEA's decision on whether or not to proceed with statutory assessment.

Stage 5: Completion of statutory assessment

This stage is reached when the LEA has agreed that there is prima facie evidence for statutory assessment and has collected advice from the professionals mentioned above. The LEA then has one of two options:

1. To conclude that the child's needs can be met from the resources already available at school; or,
2. To determine to provide the child with a Statement of Special Educational Needs.

If the LEA chooses the first option it will provide a note in lieu of a Statement of Special Educational Needs. This will detail the child's special educational needs and the provision needed to meet them, including broad educational objectives and other requirements deemed necessary. Other reports and other evidence submitted during the statutory assessment will also be made available to the parents. However, the main difference between options 1 and 2 is that in the former the provision to be made has to come from resources already available to the school. The aim in both cases will, however, be the same: to provide and meet the child's needs, as identified, fully and appropriately.

With option 2, the LEA provides a Statement of Special Educational Needs. This is a legal document which is in six sections. Section I lists the biographical details. Section II details the special educational needs, including the child's strengths and weaknesses, levels of functioning and a summary of the child's requirements. Section III focuses on the special education provision to be made, including details of broad teaching objectives, the level of staffing support to be made available and the monitoring and review arrangements. Section IV specifies the school or other arrangement required by the child, including the name of the school. Section V details the non-educational needs and Section VI deals with any provision required, e.g. physiotherapy, speech therapy.

Stage 5 and beyond

It cannot be too strongly stressed that at Stage 5 and beyond there are clear responsibilities on schools to provide for children with special educational needs, especially when these are reinforced in a Statement of Special Educational Needs. Statements, when provided, represent legal documents, the bases of contracts between the LEA and the school with the parents and child with special educational needs. The requirements contained within them must be fully understood and provided by the relevant parties. Arrangements must also be made to report on progress, normally within the structure of the annual reviews. These are formal meetings designed to revise and update statements whilst at the same time report on progress achieved.

CHAPTER 6

Statutory assessment

Introduction

There will be a number of children who do not make satisfactory progress, in spite of remedial teaching and support over the long term. This is estimated to be around 2 per cent of the school population and represents those with the most severe, long term or complex needs. Their identification, assessment and the eventual level of help they are provided with, will vary according to a number of circumstances, the most significant of which are:

● the school they are in and its approach to providing for special educational needs;

● the level of teacher expertise and resources available, including voluntary help;

● the support the child derives from parents and others;

● the actual needs of the child.

Teacher tasks

Teachers would be expected to demonstrate systematic planning and teaching if there is any intention of a child being referred to the LEA for statutory assessment. This is expected at all stages and is particularly important at Stage 4, when a decision is being made that the child's needs are so significant and complex as to call for a multi-disciplinary assessment under the 1993 Education Act. Given that teachers would need to advise the 'responsible person', i.e. the person responsible for special educational needs in the school, they would need to ensure that they are able to provide sound reasoning, with evidence to support their request for statutory assessment. It would not be sufficient to assert that the child is not learning or progressing. Instead, it would need to be demonstrated how and why the child is failing to progress within all the arrangements that have been made available. Referring back to the stages, it is clear that significant and intensive levels of support would have been made available, including specialist advice outside of the school. Therefore, a sound appreciation of the criteria which apply at Stage 4 and beyond is required if an effective response is to be achieved. It will be noted that decisions regarding requests for statutory assessment rest with the LEA, whose officers will be guided by factors pertaining to the child as well as circumstances within and beyond school.

Criteria for statutory assessment

The following questions are likely to be asked when assessing the need for statutory assessment.

The child

1. When was the child identified as having a learning difficulty and what has been his response over time, to teaching and other intervention?

2. Are there baselines recorded as to what the child can and cannot do? For example, can the child now walk, talk, read, and write, at a level that he could not do at the appropriate developmental stages? Are the child's abilities, as measured, at or below the second centile, e.g. in terms of cognitive abilities – memory, reasoning, problem solving? Or does reading, spelling and number ability fall significantly below that expected for a child of his age? What are the child's National Curriculum attainments? Is there a significant discrepancy between those, and what would normally be expected from his peers?

3. What is the child's level of maturity with regard to social, emotional and moral development? Is the child safe in a school environment, can he be trusted outside without constant supervision? Is the child a danger to himself and to others? Is the child socially and emotionally well adjusted? Is he able to integrate with peers and within school generally? Is the child easily misled or made the scapegoat? Is the child confident, articulate, able to express his point of view, or withdrawn, nervous, unusually shy and reticent?

4. What are the child's self-help and physical skills, and independence with regard to feeding, toileting? Can the child change for P.E., tie own shoelaces, participate in physical activities? Or is he slow, clumsy, prone to falls and vulnerable? Does the child require a differentiated sequence of activities that take into account his physical and safety needs? Is the child able to manage steps, stairs, distance? Is he safe with equipment?

5. Does the child have any medical problems? Does he have epilepsy or asthma? What physical activities need care in the light of these, e.g. excessive exertion, swimming, climbing? Is medication and/or physiotherapy required at regular intervals during the day, e.g. for cystic fibrosis, cerebral palsy? What are the child's needs for privacy and can the school provide for these?

6. What are the curriculum requirements? Can these be reasonably differentiated by task and by outcome?

The teacher

1. What arrangements have been made in the past to support the child's teaching, and how effective have these been? What changes are required and can these be made within the school's existing resources?

2. What are the immediate tasks, demands and pressures on the teacher? Do these make it unrealistic to provide the kinds of programmes required by the child?

3. Does the teacher have the level of experience and/or expertise required,

including the confidence to provide for the child's needs? For example, many teachers need reassurance and support – including advice, training and guidance – if they are to successfully deal with a learning difficulty outside of their range of expertise. This is often the case with mainstream teachers confronted with the problems of autism or mutism in the classroom, or when dealing with children with speech and language disorders requiring signing and other forms of non-verbal communication. The integration of children with severe learning difficulties in the mainstream, e.g. Down's Syndrome or tubero sclerosis also creates challenges (see Ware, 1994; Buckley and Bird, 1994).

The school

1. Does the school have demonstrated expertise in the area or a strong track record of innovation and successful initiatives, including strong leadership with regard to special educational needs?

2. Are resources already targeted to the school for a specific purpose? Is it a resourced school for children with either physical disabilities or visual or hearing impairment? This will only affect the decision for statutory assessment if the child is already at the school and say, requires a lift or special tables, i.e the facilities would ordinarily have been available without a statement being necessary. It should not enter the equation if it means the school needing to reallocate resources, e.g. close circuit tv provided for children with statements, or teaching inputs from specialist teachers available from special units on campus.

3. What are the special needs resources already delegated to the school? What is each special needs child's entitlement? Alternatively, how are special needs resources organised – to provide for smaller classes, small teaching groups or extra special needs staffing?

The LEA

1. What arrangements does the LEA already have in order to support a specific type of special need? Does it already provide a specialist team of teacher advisers?

2. What flexibilities exist in terms of funding, advice or placement, to provide for children whose difficulties are not likely to be long term, severe or complex?

3. What are the requirements of local schools with respect to provision for a specific type of need? How can these be jointly provided or facilitated between schools to make effective use of resources, where, for example, the needs of a hearing or visually impaired child requiring special facilities are such that it would not make economic sense to make adjustments for that child alone?

4. Does it make sense to maintain a specific pool of expertise to service specific areas of needs for schools to buy in, e.g. specialist teachers for language or for specific learning difficulties?

Teachers would need to be aware of the above criteria in order to be able to submit evidence and professional advice in support of statutory assessment. LEAs normally provide guidance on the information required and the forms used to either request statutory assessment or provide Educational Advice (called The Appendix D) including a structure which could be usefully followed.

Some LEAs have moved forward combining the request for statutory assessment and the provision of Educational Advice into one step. This saves duplicating work but has the following implications.

- the advice submitted must be clear, comprehensive, accurate and up to date, supported with concrete, objective evidence of the child's learning difficulties and the interventions attempted, with details of the outcome.
- there are some essential requirements to be met:
  - The school needs to provide a summary of the steps taken to support the child at Stages 1 to 3. These should include information relating to the nature of the management approaches adopted, how the curriculum was differentiated and the monitoring arrangements used, including the educational outcome achieved.
  - A balanced picture of the child's functioning in all areas is needed. This means including details of the child's strengths and weaknesses, interests and aptitudes. These need not be confined to school only – a child may excel at athletics but struggle with reading.
  - Comparative assessments are needed. How does the child compare with his peers? What objective information and assessments exist to show how he is performing in comparison with his peers?
  - An indication of the child's and parent's views including information relating to any special circumstances.
  - Details of health, welfare, attendance, and other information which may be appropriate. Have other professionals been involved? If so, what are their views?

Decisions relating to statutory assessment will be based on whether or not the school requires resources, 'additional to, or otherwise different from' the facilities ordinarily available. These facilities include funds already delegated to cater for children at Stages 1 to 3. Some LEAs (e.g. Hampshire) have delegated resources for this purpose, based on a Special Educational Needs Audit (see L6 under Hampshire publications in References and Further Reading Section). Others may have adopted a 'banding system' whereby resources are allocated according to the Stage the child has reached. There is no real difference in either approach as, in essence, resources are matched to the level of need based on a predetermined formula. Teachers, however, need to be aware of the agreed practices in their LEAs as requests for statutory assessment will not normally be successful unless it can be demonstrated that resources additional to or different from those available at Stages 1 to 3 are needed.

Preparation and submission of the Educational Advice (Appendix D)

It can be seen that an Appendix D requires a great deal of preparation, care and thought. It should not be entertained until the required evidence and documentation can be marshalled into a logical, coherent argument which shows exactly why statutory assessment is necessary.

The following provides a suggested checklist ranging from the pre-requirements to completion of the Appendix D.

Pre-requirements

The main problems which sometimes arise relate to:
- omission of any evaluation of the school based steps and stages and the absence of relevant documentation, a problem which should be resolved with

the introduction of Individual Education Plans.

• an inclination to proceed too early and too quickly to the next step of considering statutory assessment. This is understandable when the child is clearly perceived not to be progressing and when inadequacies of resources are considered to be at fault. However, attempts to adjust plans, arrangements and curricula may in future be required, falling in with the stages required by the Code of Practice.

• a confusion with the definition of terms. The most common and problematic relates to the school's perceptions and responses to the LEA's invitation to comment on the 'resources and provision' required by the child. This is inevitably perceived as requiring a comment on the level of staffing required.

• strong recommendations about alternative provision, which have had the effect of raising parental expectations and often pre-empting the whole assessment procedure.

It is not difficult to understand why some schools respond in the way they do – which is perfectly logical when viewed from their perspective. Their circumstances are urgent and pressing and, after all, they have the responsibility of delivering the goods to the child already *in situ*. However, they need to ensure that the problems listed in the foregoing paragraph do not arise. This will serve to reduce delay and ensure that their requirements are processed more speedily. The Code makes it a clear requirement for the LEA to specify in Section IV of the statement the level of additional assistance to be made available to the child in terms of teaching or special needs assistance support. This is a function for the LEA. Some already 'band' children's needs in categories relating to specified levels and quantities for support. Others rely on advice from their professional advisers, including schools.

A common problem relates to the process of quantification which is extremely complex. The temptation is to opt for the ideal situation in the absence of a detailed breakdown of the requirements relating to the purpose to which additional help is to be used. There have been, of course, guidelines from the DFE (Circular 11/90). These attempt to provide a formula against which resources can be determined: for example, 0.1 Qualified Teacher Assistance (QTA) and 0.1 Special Needs Assistance for a child with moderate learning difficulties, and minor deviations from this range for children with severe learning difficulties or with emotional and behavioural difficulties. These were, of course, for guidance only, with adjustments to be made once a definite view has been formed of the needs of the child on completion of the statutory assessment.

This implies that:
• careful consideration is given to the nature and extent of the child's learning difficulties, including his educational circumstances and those which pertain in the school.
• the decision relating to the quantification of resources should be made at the very end of the statutory assessment to enable a complete view of the difficulties, following examination of all the perspectives included in the Appendices. It follows that this must not be pre-empted by decisions being taken too early.

Some problems which have arisen in the past have been related to the recommendation of a level of support in appendices, not confirmed on completion of assessment. This is often related to a number of reasons, amongst which are:

- the requirement on the LEA to make efficient and effective use of its resources;
- the commitment to pursue a policy of integration;
- the requirement to be accountable for public funds and to determine the precise requirement in hours relating to the support of children in schools.

The task for schools

Schools could assist this process by clearly defining their proposals in the Appendix D. They could detail:

- the type and frequency of the educational programmes they are proposing as their intervention;
- the type of material they would need to prepare, e.g. for a child with a visual impairment;
- the safety arrangements that are necessary, e.g. around the school, in the playground, during P.E., in Science;
- the consultation and review arrangements.

This information can then be considered with the rest in the other appendices to determine the likely frequency, intensity, duration and implementation of the interventions necessary. The danger that may result by one party specifying too soon the level of support is inadequate resourcing because other problems were not known except by other contributors. There is also the problem of raising expectations and the possibility of the information being used to apportion blame if the child fails to make the expected progress. This is becoming quite frequent, forming parental responses to annual review where they feel, strongly and with some justification, that their child's chances of progress have been denied because of inadequate resourcing compared to what was recommended by one professional.

Finally, the other main and very frequent complication that tends to occur relates to the type of provision a child needs. Teachers sometimes feel that a child is inappropriately placed in their school for particular reasons. Whilst this is acceptable, the issue becomes confounded when generalisations are made, based on inadequate evidence. The most common error is to assume that a child who has not coped in one school will have the same problems elsewhere if the type of establishment is similar. Difficulties which have often resulted when making specific placement recommendations have been in terms of:

- shutting doors to the child with regard to securing an alternative placement;
- constraining the authority into making one type of placement as opposed to another;
- denying parental choice;
- opening the possibility for litigation on the basis that the child's future has been prejudiced.

The following Case Study illustrates this.

Case Study

Jane is an 11 year old who was recently issued with a Statement of Special Educational Needs. Her Appendix D says that she has emotional and behavioural difficulties, making it unlikely that she will be able to cope in the mainstream. The other appendices do not support this and therefore the Statement, whilst acknowledging that Jane has difficulties, proposes that her needs should continue to be met in the mainstream. A number of objectives have been set and additional support in the form of special needs assistance has been agreed.

However, Jane has been refused a place at her local secondary school to which she was to transfer in the following term and the LEA has been asked to intervene by the parents. The headteacher of the secondary school is concerned that his primary colleagues have advised against continuation in the mainstream and he has the full support of his governing body. On the other hand, the parents argue that none of the other contributors see the need for a placement other than in the mainstream. This includes the educational psychologist and the multi-disciplinary body which sat on the LEA's behalf to confirm that placement in the mainstream is appropriate. This case remains to be resolved but has already been extremely costly in terms of time and the various meetings and deliberations needed. The indications are that:

● The parents will be seeking an alternative mainstream placement and ask the LEA to provide the transport.

● The alternative secondary schools will also be refusing admission either on the grounds that the child's local school should seriously reconsider or on the grounds that they too feel mainstream education is out of the question. In any event, the parents no longer want anything more to do with their local schools, both the primary and secondary schools, feeling aggrieved with them.

● The LEA finds itself in the position of having to find a solution acceptable to all parties. Therefore, what started as a genuine concern about how to provide for Jane has backfired to the extent that she may be still without a school place at the start of her secondary education.

This case, although unresolved, serves to highlight how genuine concerns can backfire and cause a 'ripple effect' with unexpected consequences. A lesson that should be learned is the vulnerability of parents and the child in respect of recommendations and decisions made by third parties, sometimes with dire consequences concerning their future. Extreme care should be taken to avoid pre-empting the outcome of the statutory assessment; this will avoid confusion, conflict and uncertainty, which only serve to cause delays and work against the child's best interests.

Conclusions

Statutory assessments represent complex procedures. Parents with little or no knowledge of these procedures may find the process daunting and will be anxious to ensure that they are able to safeguard their child's best interests. Knowing how best to contribute and to collaborate on equal terms would be a challenge many of them would wish to be setting themselves and it would be helpful for them to have every assistance to succeed. This is where the LEA's Named Person will have a useful role, particularly in regard to explaining the processes to be followed, including details of parental rights at each stage. Help could also be available from the Named Person/Friend or adviser to the parents.

Together, they could be assisted to make sense of and respond effectively to the volume of documentation which follows completion of the statutory assessment procedures.

In particular, parents should be advised of their rights to:

• contribute to the assessment by providing their own Parental Advice and/or Parental Representation, which is advice prepared by a friend, relative or more frequently, professional adviser (see Glossary);

• two meetings with an officer of the LEA if they are unhappy with the contents and proposals in the draft Statement, i.e. the Statement before it is signed and finalised as a legal document;

• independent advice from their Named Person.

They should also be told of the importance of observing the time limits that apply at each stage of the assessment process, e.g. 29 days within which to submit their advice and evidence from the date of the start of statutory assessment, and 15 days between meetings at draft Statement stage.

CHAPTER 7

Annual Reviews

Purposes of
Annual Reviews

Annual Reviews are required minimally once a year in order to review and update the Statement of Special Educational Needs. More frequent reviews may be required if the child's needs change rapidly.

The main purposes of the Annual Review are to:
- review progress over the preceding year;
- identify outstanding tasks and agree future objectives, both new ones and those set previously and not completely achieved;
- review needs and update the Statement in the light of this;
- review levels of provision;
- review appropriateness of placement;
- recommend whether or not to continue to maintain the Statement.

How to get the best out
of Annual Reviews?

Annual Reviews provide an ideal opportunity to consult with parents and to formalise plans in order to continue to provide the appropriate support and help to the child. However, they can also be rather formal and daunting occasions to parents as well as teachers. When this happens, there is a valuable opportunity lost for close co-operation between both parties. An atmosphere of trust can be generated with effective and sensitive chairing of these meetings, a task often falling to the headteacher, at times assisted by the LEA representative, usually the Educational Psychologist. A great deal of work could and should also have been done beforehand to reassure parents and make them feel welcome and truly valued. If children are also invited, then the process of the meeting takes on even greater importance, greatly helped by advance planning. It should be remembered, of course, that children have a right to attend their Annual Reviews. However, the task of empowering them to make an effective contribution is daunting and a real challenge to schools. This will be covered later in this chapter.

The following is normally found helpful at Annual Reviews:

Physical arrangements

- seating to be organised beforehand to allow parents and child to sit next to each other, preferably opposite the chairperson but near to the class teacher or other person familiar to them.
- people representing authority, e.g. LEA representative, headteacher, not to bunch together.
- sitting behind desks to be avoided.
- spacious room with comfortable chairs to be preferred if available, with notice not to be disturbed once meeting has started.

Process

- chairperson introduces himself/herself and invites others to do so.
- chairperson briefly outlines agenda, including purpose of the Review and reminds all parties of contents in Sections 2 and 3 of Statement Cover, i.e. special educational needs and special educational provision.
- class teacher or headteacher gives report of objectives set previously and progress achieved.
- parents are invited to respond and express their views and thoughts on any matter which they want to share or discuss. (Most parents are articulate and able enough to contribute or even lead the meeting but there are some who need reassurance and encouragement. These parents should not be asked direct questions until they have had an opportunity to listen and to 'warm' to the discussion. There are many instances when they may feel intimidated or marginalised, needing to be brought in and actively encouraged to contribute to the meeting.)
- avoid jargon. (If any educational terminology is used, ensure that parents understand what they mean. If not, provide an explanation. This applies in particular to National Curriculum terminology which may be meaningless to parents. For example, what does it mean if a ten year old child is functioning at Level 1 of the National Curriculum?)

Requirements for Review meetings

A copy of the Statement and of the latest Annual Review, if one has been carried out, should be available at the meeting. The minimum information that will be required from these relates to:

- the child's special educational needs and the special educational provision being made; this will help to establish whether the child's special educational needs remain the same, whether some have changed and whether new ones have arisen;
- the objectives set and being worked towards; this is necessary in order to determine the extent to which progress has been made towards the achievement of these objectives;
- any written information provided by parties unable to attend the review; this should normally have been made available to the parents well in advance of the meeting.

An Agenda for schools

A useful agenda which schools might use is included in the Code of Practice. It states that the following questions should be addressed:

- What are the parents' views of the past year's progress and their aspirations for the future?
- What are the pupil's views of the past year's progress and his aspirations for the future?
- What is the school's view of the child's progress over the past year? What has been the child's progress towards meeting the overall objectives in the Statement? What success has the child achieved in meeting the targets set?
- Have there been significant changes in the child's circumstances which affect his development and progress?
- Is current provision, including the National Curriculum, or arrangements substituted for it, appropriate to the child's needs?
- What educational targets should be adopted against which the child's educational progress will be assessed during the coming year and at the next review?
- Is the Transition Plan helping the pupil's progress to adult life?
- Is any further action required and if so, by whom?
- Does the Statement remain appropriate?
- Are any amendments to the Statement required or should the LEA be recommended to cease to maintain it?

There is one problem worth noting here and this is with the ordering of the questions. In some cases, especially when parents need to warm up to the meeting, it would be more appropriate to start with teachers and others detailing their views and informing parents and the child that they will have an opportunity to respond and comment afterwards. If need be, they may even ask immediately for clarification of any point or issue.

Agenda for parents

In asking parents to give their 'views of the past year's progress and their aspirations for the future', the following simplification may be found helpful by all parties:

- what progress has been noted by parents in the past year in respect of
  - behaviour and relationships
  - interest and motivation
  - attitude to learning
  - co-operation with parents at home
  - perseverance with tasks
  - attainments and skills development;
- what has pleased them;
- what continues to cause them concern and any suggestions to deal with this;
- any significant events which might have affected their child's progress;
- what they would like to see achieved during the next year.

Parents can be forewarned about the type of questions they would be asked, with advice and guidance in respect of the contributions expected of them. Some authorities, e.g. Hampshire, produces an Annual Review leaflet which explains the Annual Review in sufficient detail to enable effective parental contribution.

Essential issues to be addressed at Annual Reviews

The Annual Review should, at minimum, cover the following.

The past

- Exactly what progress has been achieved during the past year?
- How does the intervention provided match with the needs identified in the Statement?
- How appropriate were the teaching objectives which were set and have they been achieved? If so, to what extent?
- Have outcomes been measured and recorded?

The present

- What are the most important needs of the child now and in what priority order?
- What needs to be done, by whom, by when and how?
- Is there anything new that has come to light and how best to plan and provide for this?
- What constitute short and medium term targets and can these be agreed?

The future

- What are the long term plans for the child?
  - independent study skills, co-operative behaviour, fluent and accurate reading and spelling
  - attainment targets comparable to the child's peers, GCSE success
  - development of life skills, independence, social skills
  - vocational placement, work employment.

Recommendations to the LEA and parents

This relates essentially to the following:
- Are the child's needs being appropriately met?
- Does the school placement remain appropriate?
- Is there any change needed in the nature or level of the special educational provision?
- Does the Statement need to be maintained?

Including children at their Annual Review meetings

Children have a right to attend their Annual Reviews and should therefore be included as far as possible. It is, however, acknowledged that there are some difficulties and concerns to be addressed if their inclusion is to be effective and not counter productive. These arise when:
- information to be discussed at Annual Reviews is of a highly sensitive nature, best not fully disclosed to the child, e.g. a terminal illness, predicted consequences of other medical diagnoses in terms of learning and/or physical deterioration or any uncertainties which are likely to cause unnecessary worry and anxiety to the child;
- reports to be discussed contain information which may have a harmful effect on the child's self-image and self-esteem or which could cause unnecessary

embarrassment, e.g. ability levels, unsociable behaviour;

- parents or other parties wish to have time to share information in confidence in order to minimise the risk of causing anxiety, embarrassment or distress to the child.

However, when the above applies, it should be possible to include the child in the deliberations of the Annual Review, with some adjustments and fine tuning in relation to the timing, duration of attendance, preparation for and support at the meeting. The more able and confident the child, the more effective they are likely to be at their Reviews.

In preparing children for Annual Reviews, the following is helpful:

1. Explain to the child well beforehand that there is to be a meeting about how he is being helped in school, i.e. remove the focus from the child's weaknesses and emphasise the strategies in operation.

2. Explain that the parents are being invited to attend.

3. Provide guidance to parents as to how their child is being prepared for the Annual Review so that they can help too, by being consistent in their approach and in the way they share information.

4. Tell the child how many adults will be at the review and who they are. Explain what is expected of the child and reassure by explaining how they are to be supported. Explain that they may contribute as much or as little as they wish and that they may choose just to listen to the discussion and proposals.

5. Explain the procedure as clearly as possible – what happens, why it is necessary to look at reports/statements, how long the meeting lasts, which part they will be attending. Avoid jargon and explain in language understandable to the child such terms as Statement, Annual Review, objectives and provision.

6. Explain that their point of view matters and that they are not expected to necessarily agree with what is being said. They can ask for clarification on any point or indeed challenge any inaccuracy. They can also suggest ways in which they would like to work or be helped.

7. Prepare the child for the kinds of questions to be asked at the Review. Explain what these mean and the kinds of information being looked for.

8. Ascertain the child's views and relay these on his behalf, if he is unable or unwilling to do so at the meeting. Ensure that they are willing for this to happen prior to the meeting.

9. Do not keep children waiting. Include them at the beginning and, unless they wish to attend the whole meeting, tell them how long they will be attending for.

10. Explain that they will have full information from their parents and teachers in respect of decisions made at the meeting if they are not able to be present for the whole proceedings. Also, that where parents are unable to be present, a Named Person, friend or advocate can represent them.

Annual Review documentation

As should be clear by now, there are some clear requirements needed for effective Annual Reviews. The documentation that arise from these are as important, representing the only records of the meeting. This information, if properly collected and recorded, provides an extremely useful planning document which should be kept 'live and active', influencing teaching and any other action throughout the year during which they remain in force. However, their completion can be daunting to the inexperienced and a specimen Annual Review example is given at the end of this chapter.

Annual Reviews and school reports

The question is often asked by teachers as to whether it is best to combine the Annual Review with the school report to parents. This is in an attempt to reduce the time required in administration and production of these reports in addition to the necessary meetings with parents. In considering the best response, it is helpful to remember that the Annual Review is a legal requirement and serves the specific purpose of reviewing the child's Statement of Special Educational Needs. As such, it needs to focus on the information contained in the Statement in relation to needs, provision, teaching objectives, the child's and the parents' views. This is required for evaluation and decision making and does not need to go into the level of detail which can be included in a school report. At the secondary stage in particular, subject teachers may wish to comment in detail on the child's achievements in their subject area in the school report. This will not be necessary in an Annual Review report, except to indicate the level of the child's attainments, especially if it is in a subject which is not causing concern and which is not a point of focus in the Statement. Similarly, whilst it may be important to comment at length in the Annual Review on say, how a literacy problem is being addressed, this will be inappropriate in a school report.

When attempting to combine the information required for the Annual Review and school report, the task is often compromised. There is also the problem of timing. The school report is not normally required until the end of the year. The Annual Review report has to be produced on each anniversary of the statement. It may therefore be preferable, depending on which one is required first, to keep the processes separate but make clear to parents that the information will be used in both reports, as appropriate. For instance, if a school report produced in July contains valuable information about the child's attainments and needs in various areas, there is no reason why this should not be built upon for the purpose of the Annual Review if this were to follow in the Autumn term.

ANNUAL REVIEW REPORT (Specimen)

Name: Dan   Date of Birth 1.12.84

Address:
Names of Parents/Person responsible:
School: NC Year:
Class teacher/Tutor:
Date of Statement/Last Annual Review:
Date of Current Annual Review Meeting:

Details of existing provision from (a) school (b) LEA (c) other agencies:

Please list those invited to the Annual Review Meeting. Please indicate with an (A) those who attended, any reasons given for non-attendance, and tick who provided written contributions.

Name   *Position/Relationship*   *Additional Information*

1. *Previously Identified Needs*

(a) *Special Educational Needs: from Statement/last Annual Review*
      1. Language difficulties, particularly in respect of verbal communication skills.
      2. Weak literacy skills, especially writing and spelling.
      3. Weak numeracy skills, especially number operations.
      4. Low confidence and self-esteem.
      5. Weak study skills.
      6. Weak motor skills.

(b) *Non-educational needs: from Statement/last Annual Review*
      1. Asthmatic – problems with school attendance due to poor health.

(c) Overall objectives from Statement/last Annual Review

To enable Dan to improve:

       1. Language and communication skills.

       2. Reading and writing development.

       3. Numeracy development.

       4. Confidence and self-esteem.

       5. Study skills.

       6. Motor skills.

(d) Targets set and worked towards since Statement issued/last Annual Review (see section 1(a) Special Educational Needs)

1.1: Encourage Dan to contribute to small group/class discussion.

1.2 : Improve listening and attention skills to ensure improved comprehension and retention of key information.

2.1: Improve reading accuracy, reading comprehension, reading fluency and speed, by approximately 6 to 9 months.

3.1: Develop number competence through mastery of the four rules of number.

3.2: Encourage and improve use of calculator.

3.3: Develop understanding and competence with fractions and decimals.

4.1: Enable Dan to have regular, planned opportunities for success in his work and to give him feedback on a daily basis.

4.2: Encourage Dan to participate in group work which is planned in such a way as to make him feel listened to and valued.

5.1: Improve concentration and attention skills through structured tasks, systematically planned and implemented.

5.2: Encourage Dan to actively extract information in his reading and discussions, to make notes, and record his work for future reference.

5.3: Help plan a structured and realistic time plan for study during school hours.

6.1: Improve hand/eye co-ordination and, more specifically, to encourage the development of

– fine motor and co-ordination skills, including threading, throwing, aiming and catching skills;

– handwriting through the development of a cursive script.

2. *Report on Progress over Last Year*
(a) Strengths

1. Excellent auditory short term memory.
2. Developing handwriting.
3. Gaining confidence in all aspects of school life.
4. Enthusiastic.
5. Able to share feelings and experiences with a group.
6. Polite, well-mannered and displays good behaviour.

(b) Extent to which objectives outlined in 1(c) and targets set in 1(b) have been met:

1. Language and communication skills

Dan now speaks confidently in front of a group, whether taking a part in a play or presenting a poem. He has a much improved vocabulary and is able to communicate his thoughts effectively and with clarity.

2. Reading and writing development

Dan has made gains of approximately six months in respect of reading and spelling accuracy. Reading comprehension is also much improved, as is legibility and speed of writing.

3. Numeracy development

Dan has made progress across the curriculum, most recently in Maths AT2 'number' and mental calculation.

4. Confidence and self-esteem

Dan has settled well at R L School, making several friends and becoming a popular class member. He has responded to the small, structured and supportive environment where he has been able to experience success in a number of areas, both in his social relationships and with the curriculum.

5. Study skills

Dan is interested and works consistently in all subject areas. He shows good application to his work and is keen to improve and succeed. He is to be encouraged to:

– Improve his concentration span from 10 to 15 minutes.

– Improve his speed of work, including its presentation.

– Demonstrate more originality and creativity in his writing.

– Identify and extract the key issues in dealing with different types of information.

– Develop effective strategies to improve his access to the curriculum.

6. Motor skills

The P.E. programme and practical subject areas provide Dan with opportunities to develop his motor skills. These will be used to improve:

– Fine motor skills, e.g. hand/eye co-ordination,

manipulative skills.

– Gross motor skills, including balance, physical agility, spatial awareness.

(c) Factors identified as affecting the achievement of objectives (i.e. significant change in the pupil's circumstances)

Dan's attendance at school is now much improved, following the change in his medication to control his asthma. His circumstances are also more settled at home, so he is generally happier and more able to devote time to his studies. His older brother, with whom he used to share a room, has moved out and he can now work quietly and without interruption in the evenings and weekends.

3. National Curriculum

(a) Teacher assessment of profiles of the current levels of attainment in the National Curriculum core subjects

Subject	Level Achieved	Level Working On
English		
Speaking and listening	2	2/3
Reading	2	2/3
Writing	1	2
Spelling	1	2
Handwriting	1	2
Mathematics		
Using and applying	2	3
Number	2	3
Algebra	2	3
Measure	2	3
Shape and space	2	3
Handling data	2	3
Overall levels experienced in Science		
Scientific investigations	2	3
Life and living processes	2	3
Materials and their processes	2	3
Physical processes	2	3

(b) Details of any modifications, disapplications or arrangements made to deliver a broad and balanced curriculum

It has been possible to deliver the full National Curriculum through a systematic, differentiated teaching approach within small groups of no more than fouteen.

(c) Extent to which the National Curriculum, or any arrangements substituted for the National Curriculum, has been effective

61

Dan has been achieving at around Level 2 of the National Curriculum in the core areas (see detailed breakdown). The relevant Attainment Targets have been broken down into small steps, taught within a systematic, sequential approach, with the emphasis on overlearning and skill consolidation.

4. *Special Educational Needs*

(a) New needs which were not recorded on the Statement

Dan shows some artistic ability and talent and is to be entered for GCSE.

(b) Needs recorded on the Statement which are no longer present

Speech and language difficulties as recorded on Statement are not such severe weaknesses and no longer call for speech therapy.

(c) Summary of current special educational needs in the light of the Review: Special Educational Needs

1. Moderate learning difficulties.

2. Language, literacy and numeracy difficulties.

3. Physical and co-ordination problems.

(d) Summary of current non-educational needs in the light of the Review

1. Asthma – which is now well controlled by medication.

5. *Recommendations for the coming year*

Specific targets for the coming year:

(a) Short term objectives

Dan will

1. Make oral presentations for at least 2 minutes and up to 5 minutes.

2. Participate in silent reading and group reading for a total of 20 minutes daily.

3. Further improve the legibility and speed of his handwriting.

4. Engage in selected maths activities and use a calculator when appropriate.

5. Engage in estimating and checking tasks of increasing difficulty.

6. Succeed in the tasks he is allocated, at least 50 per cent of the time, to maintain his enthusiasm and build on his confidence.

7. Maintain high standards in attendance, and thought for others.

(b) Long term objectives

1. Improved language and communication skills, as shown in clarity, confidence and competence in his communications.

2. Greater independence with learning and other tasks as assessed on agreed measures between him and his teacher.

3. Achieve full potential in curriculum areas and in particular to:

– develop basic literacy and numeracy skills, with improvements of between 6 to 9 months in a school year;

– attain Level 3 of the National Curriculum in the core areas in the coming year.

4. Achieve at least Grade C in his Art GCSE.

5. Undertake vocational training and experience for two weeks, full time.

6. Be offered an appropriate post-16 placement.

(c) How will the provision available be used to meet these targets?

1. Small teaching groups.

2. Supportive, structured teaching/learning environment.

3. Differentiated work and materials.

4. Individual programmes, tackling recognised weaknesses.

(d) How will the non-educational provision available be used to meet these targets?

None specifically allocated. However, some support will be offered in order to help with attendance and confidence building.

(e) Any additional National Curriculum arrangements including any modifications or disapplication of the National Curriculum. In the case of disapplication the provision proposed to be substituted to maintain a broad and balanced curriculum

None

6. Pupil's views

Dan feels that he has made consistent progress in his work and is particularly pleased with his Art work. He would like to have continuing help with literacy and is keen to take books home to practise his reading skills.

This has been a good year for Dan. He feels healthier and more able to maintain regular attendance at school. He is also more able to participate in physical activities and is gaining confidence all round. Dan says he is very happy in school, having made many friends with his teachers and his peers.

7. Views of Parents/Person Responsible

Mr and Mrs G are pleased that Dan is so well settled in school. They are relieved that his medication seems to be controlling his asthma and feel sure that his more regular attendance will enable him to sustain progress. Both parents are now able to spend time with Dan and help him with his work without distraction.

8. Conclusions and Recommendations to the LEA

Have the pupil's needs changed significantly since the last Annual Review?   Yes/No

9. Is a change in the level or nature of educational non-educational provision recommended?   Yes/No

10. Is the pupil's current placement inappropriate for the coming year?   Yes/No

If the answer to any of the above questions is 'Yes', please specify the amendment to the Statement you are recommending. Make reference to attached reports which support your recommendation.

11. Does a Statement need to be maintained   Yes/No

If the answer is 'No', you are recommending that the LEA ceases to maintain the Statement. It is important, therefore, that there is evidence that this has been fully discussed at the Annual Review meeting.

Proposed date of next Annual Review Meeting:

Report prepared by: (please print)

Headteacher's signature: Date:

CHAPTER 8

Year 9 Reviews and Transition Plans

The Year 9 reviews replace the previous statutory assessments at ages $13^1/_2$ to $14^1/_2$. They effectively represent two reviews, carried out in tandem. The first is normally the school's responsibility and follows the usual annual review format. The second is very much the LEA's responsibility as it has to prepare and produce the Transition Plan within one week of the review meeting. However, it is up to the school, parents and agencies represented to ensure an accurate assessment of what is required to be incorporated in the Transition Plan and, with this in mind, a specimen Plan is provided at the end of the chapter, together with some guidelines as to completion.

The Purpose of the Transition Plan

The Transition Plan is intended to be a comprehensive document compiled to enable the smooth transition of the young person from school to adult life. It spans the final years of schooling and can be conveniently divided into the following time frames:

1. The final two years of schooling, i.e. 14 to 16.

2. The years following transfer from school to college, training or employment, i.e. 16 to 19.

3. Transfer to higher education, further training or continuing employment, i.e. 19 to 21.

4. The 'adult' years, especially when the person needs support with independence, employment or the active involvement and support of Social Services, e.g. with respect to care plans or funding for care arrangements.

Consequently, it is important that the Transition Plan is regularly reviewed and updated to ensure that the needs identified and issues raised are kept in focus and remain under active consideration. This will not happen unless proposals are clearly defined and tasks are clearly agreed and allocated, with arrangements built in to monitor progress, check on outstanding issues and trigger action. This will require liaising with and involving relevant parties at all stages, i.e. not only at the time of the 14+ Review but at all subsequent reviews and planning meetings.

The Transition Plan should therefore include an action plan which clearly specifies:
- the action required
- the people responsible
- the time frames being worked to
- the indicators to be used to monitor performance and measure progress in respect of the action agreed at the Transition Plan and subsequent meetings.

The tasks of schools in relation to Year 9 reviews and Transition Plan meetings:

The key tasks for schools are to:
- discharge their obligations as specified in the young person's Statement of Special Educational Needs, in addition to the objectives agreed at the 14+ Review.
- activate the Transition Plan and keep the action agreed under regular review.
- work closely with key agencies such as the LEA, Social Services Departments and the Careers Service in order to progress plans.
- provide point of reference/contact to outside agencies until such time as some other agency takes over.
- check that plans are being followed; if not, chase up whoever is responsible for action.
- maintain contact with young person and/or parents and keep them informed of progress or of any plans outstanding.

The role of Statutory Agencies

1. The LEA
The LEA *must*:
- organise the 14+ Review;
- invite the Careers Service;
- produce the Transition Plan from information which is factual and accurate, as far as possible presenting the young person in a positive light;
- inform Social Services of the date of the meeting;
- and school leaving date for a young person who is considered disabled.

The LEA should also:
- invite the Careers Service to future Reviews;
- inform the Further Education Funding Council of any special arrangements;
- only pass on information to relevant parties, with the consent of the young person and his parents.

2. The Social Services Department

The Social Services Department *must*:
- carry out a multi-disciplinary assessment and produce care plans for children

and adults with significant special needs;

- make arrangements for people over 18 years of age if they have required help from this department prior to their eighteenth birthday;
- give the young person choice, on whether to accept or refuse assessment and help under the terms of the Disabled Person's Act, 1986.

3. The Role of Professional Advisers:

Professional advisers include those employed by the LEA or statutory agencies, e.g. educational psychologists, doctors, careers advisers and social workers. They can also be engaged by parents and are not restricted to those currently involved as others may be called in as the need arises.

Their main tasks are to:

- determine the young person's needs;
- help formulate the plan without pre-empting the action;
- accept responsibilities which are within and not outside their remit;
- facilitate the consultation and meeting process;
- provide advice on professional issues within their expertise.

A checklist of the issues to be addressed, including an action list for this group, is provided in Appendix 8.

How to prepare a Transition Plan

The Code of Practice provides guidance on the questions to be addressed in the preparation of a Transition Plan. These are broken down into four sections dealing with the:

- role of the school;
- responsibilities and contributions of professionals;
- expectations and involvement of parents;
- hopes, aspirations and needs of the young person.

The questions

The questions included in the Code of Practice are reproduced below.

The school

- What are the young person's curriculum needs during transition? How can the curriculum help the young person to play his role in the community; make use of leisure and recreational facilities; assume new roles in the family; develop new educational and vocational skills?

The professionals

- Which new professionals need to be involved in planning for transition: for example, occupational psychologists, a rehabilitation medicine specialist, occupational and other therapists?
- How can they develop close working relationships with colleagues in other agencies to ensure effective and coherent plans for the young person in transition?
- Does the young person have any special health or welfare needs which will

require planning and support from health and social services now or in the future?

● Are assessment arrangements for transition clear, relevant and shared between all agencies concerned?

● How can information best be transferred from children's to adult services to ensure a smooth transitional arrangement?

● Where a young person requires a particular technological aid, do the arrangements for transition include appropriate training and arrangements for securing technological support?

● Is education after the age of 16 appropriate, and if so, at school or at a college of further education?

The family

● What do parents expect of their son's or daughter's adult life?

● What can they contribute in terms of helping their child develop personal and social skills, an adult life style and acquire new skills?

● Will parents experience new care needs and require practical help in terms of aids, adaptations or general support during these years?

The young person

● What information do young people need in order to make informed choices?

● What local arrangements exist to provide advocacy and advice if required?

● How can young people be encouraged to contribute to their own Transition Plan and make positive decisions about the future?

● If young people are living away from home or attending a residential school outside their own LEA, are there special issues relating to the location of services when they leave school which should be discussed in planning?

● What are the young person's hopes and aspirations for the future, and how can these be met?

Responding to the questions

The school

What are the young person's curriculum needs during transition? This question is more easily answered by reference to the Year 9 Annual Review and after discussion has taken place with the young person and his parents as to what their proposals are for the future. The important point is the young person's needs during transition, i.e. at 14+, which represents the final two years in school and before transfer to further education. The emphasis, therefore, depends on the priorities and objectives agreed at the 14+ Review. Consideration also needs to be given to the following:

1. Given the time available, which skills/subject areas are to be given priority whilst at the same time providing a broadly based, balanced curriculum?

2. How does the curriculum prepare the child for transition and how relevant is it to the options to be pursued at 16+ ?

If the young person's intentions for the future are known, identifying the curriculum needs is fairly straightforward. For instance, a disabled 14 year old who is keen on a career in television or journalism would probably find the inclusion of word processing, dictating and communication skills in the curriculum to be useful preparation and training. Similarly, an able-bodied 14 year old with aspirations to enter engineering would do better to include technical and science subjects in their courses of study. The key is to ascertain in which direction the young person is heading. This, combined with an assessment of his strengths and weaknesses, together with an evaluation of the career opportunities likely to be open to the young person, should facilitate and guide planning of the curriculum areas which require emphasis and coverage at this stage of education. New 'skills gaps' may be identified, or long standing weaknesses may require remediation. The provision of compensatory strategies may also need to be considered for weaknesses which are particularly resistant to teaching and improvement.

The curricular emphasis will depend on the long term aim for the young person. If it is considered that he should continue in further education and be prepared for employment, work and vocational skills will be a priority. These could include the development of timekeeping, self-organisation, punctuality, presentation and communication skills. On the other hand, if the aim is to encourage independence, then the curriculum should focus more on life skills, e.g. self-care, budgeting and shopping, menu planning and preparation and self-advocacy.

Action 1

1. Consult with young person and parents.
2. Determine career aspirations/future plans.
3. Agree curricular priorities/additions for final two years at school.

How can the curriculum help the young person to play his role in the community? The information required will relate to the skills the young person will need so as to play a meaningful and productive role in the community. For some students, this could mean development of vocational and work related skills. For others, it could mean no more than the development of life and independence skills, perhaps relating to self-care, mobility or social skills.

Action 2

1. Determine role young person is likely to play in community, e.g. employment prospects and levels of independence achievable.
2. Plan curriculum and include the teaching of skills which would be a useful preparation for transition to adult life.
3. Explore community options, such as work experience,and provide opportunities to practise skills *in situ.*

How can the curriculum help the young person make use of leisure and recreational facilities? Teachers would have already established the young person's leisure and recreational interests. It is also likely that a full programme of activities is already provided at school, which can be easily extended beyond school. For example, a young person may be actively involved in the school's sporting activities and these could easily continue as future leisure and recreational pursuits, the facilities and arrangements having already been made available. An understanding of the opportunities which the young person will benefit from in the long term helps and could quite easily focus on specific aspects of his development, e.g. physical, aesthetic, spiritual, personal or social development.

Action 3

1. Determine young person's recreational and leisure interests and review opportunities offered by school.

2. Extend and/or consolidate on recreational and leisure pursuits of long term interest or significance.

3. Make/develop links between young person, parents and leisure provider.

4. Determine and agree objectives and include in Transition Plan.

How can the curriculum help the young person to assume new roles in the family? This may not always be necessary. Many parents might feel that their teenager is already playing a full part and this would need to be recognised and acknowledged. Where this is not so, consultation with the child and his parents will be required in order to determine how and in which areas new roles are relevant and achievable. It may be that for some young persons this new role will involve assuming greater responsibility and independence for the self or for greater involvement in family activities, and this would need to be carefully ascertained with a view to determining the order of priority.

Action 4

1. Seek the views of parents and, with young person, agree role expected/appropriate within family setting.

2. Define this role and how it is to be supported.

3. Establish how progress is to be reviewed and future plans made.

How can the curriculum help the young person to develop new educational and vocational skills? This has already been touched upon in this chapter under the guidance on the young person's curriculum needs during transition. New educational skills relate to future requirements and/or current interests. A person who wishes to enter the world of travel and tourism might wish to undertake a serious study of languages. This would represent an addition of both educational and vocational skills. On the other hand, someone interested in commerce may opt for business studies and possibly learn vocational skills such as the use of computers for word processing and the production of spreadsheets and databases. The key is to identify the young person's career aspirations and match these to his educational requirements.

Action 5

1. Identify skills necessary or linked with career choice.
2. Establish most appropriate route or course for student to follow on leaving school.
3. Prepare for this within the curriculum.

The professionals

Which new professionals need to be involved in planning for transition: for example, occupational psychologists, a rehabilitation medicine specialist, occupational and other therapists? This would of course depend on the young person's special needs. Occupational psychologists are likely to be helpful in matching career choice to abilities, needs and aptitude and will be able to advise on the appropriateness or otherwise of some career aspirations. Rehabilitation medicine specialists will be needed for advice regarding children who have clear medical and/or physical needs, i.e. those continuing to require extensive medical care, including further surgery. For example, some young people may require revision of medical and other aids, e.g. for hearing, vision or mobility. Others may need continuing support with regard to chronic problems, e.g. dialysis for kidney dysfunction/failure, corrective treatment for deformities. These will require specialist medical advice and support, especially if it is proposed that the young person be moved from his home area for further education.

Occupational therapists are invaluable in the provision of advice relating to children who have physical difficulties, especially with regard to the adaptation of learning material, tools, or adjustments to be made in the living accommodation to be used. They work closely with Social Services and can act as an important link between school and this agency. Other therapists include physiotherapists whose role remains central to the support of children with severe physical problems.

Schools may find that it is difficult to ensure the attendance of some of these specialists, in which case they should liaise with a representative of the department concerned, e.g. the Clinical Medical Officer for the rehabilitation medicine specialist and the physiotherapist, the educational psychologist for the occupational psychologist, and the social worker for the occupational therapist.

Action 6

1. Decide who needs to be involved.
2. Establish contact, if not already done, and name agency.

How can they develop close working relationships with colleagues in other agencies to ensure effective and coherent plans for the young person in transition? In the majority of cases, this is likely to be through contact with school at planning and Annual Review meetings. If tasks are allocated to named parties for action and follow up, this will be one way of ensuring that communication is started and continued with the parties who require to be involved. Plans, however, will only become effective and coherent after consultation, discussion and agreement to fulfil the agreed priorities identified.

Action 7

1. The relevant agency will decide how to do this.
2. School may volunteer to be the point of contact.

Does the young person have any special health or welfare needs which will require planning and support from health and social services now or in the future? This is especially important for children with medical or social needs, including those who require sheltered accommodation, and unable to lead a completely independent life. Advance warning of their requirements should normally have taken place within the assessment required of the Social Services Department at 14+ under the terms of the Disabled Persons Act 1986. This will help provide the necessary information and alert the relevant parties to current and future requirements.

Action 8

1. Establish requirements with Health or Social Services.
2. Record these and name contacts for follow up/action.
3. If young person is disabled, seek view/ assessment of Social Services under the Disabled Persons Act 1986.

Are assessment arrangements for transition clear, relevant and shared between all agencies concerned? Until the young person leaves school, this will be the responsibility of the school, working closely with careers advisers and other agencies.

Action 9

1. Agree who is going to take lead responsibility for this.
2. Name this agency.
3. Build in monitoring/review arrangements through meetings to determine progress and action required to achieve plan.

How can information best be transferred from children's to adult services to ensure a smooth transitional arrangement? Normally, this would be done through the transfer of school records, preceded by regular communication at meetings through prior involvement of the agencies providing adult services.

> **Action 10**
>
> 1. Transfer of school records at the appropriate time.
> 2. Ensure planning requirements are undertaken well beforehand and that agencies are alerted sufficiently early.

Where a young person requires a particular technological aid, do the arrangements for transition include appropriate training and arrangements for securing technological support? An example of this would be a communication aid for children with no speech, activated through a computer. Other examples include visual and mobility aids, in which case the appropriate specialists, e.g. mobility officers, would need to be involved.

> **Action 11**
>
> 1. Establish whose responsibility it is to provide/fund the equipment/service.
> 2. Make contact with and remind parties of equipment/service needing to be in place at the time of student's transfer, if not earlier.

Is education after the age of 16 appropriate, and if so, at school or at a college of further education? This would depend on a number of factors including the current placement and facilities available. Other factors will relate to the type of course and the curricular and/or other experiences. It is likely that a great deal of this information will be directly available from the Annual Review.

> **Action 12**
>
> 1. Weigh up all available options and discuss 'pros and cons' with all parties.
> 2. Agree most appropriate option and consult with service provider, i.e. LEA or FEFC (Further Education Funding Council).
> 3. If additional costs are likely to be incurred, alert service providers in plenty of time.

The family

What do parents expect of their son's or daughter's adult life? Parents will require some help and guidance with this question. A suggested simplification is:
– What do they consider to be their child's medium to long term needs?
– What skills would they like them to develop?
– What kind of experiences are they seeking for them?
– What are their priorities in terms of preparing their child for an independent, meaningful and productive future?
Parents will be well advised to consult with their son or daughter when

answering this question.

What can they contribute in terms of helping their child develop personal and social skills, an adult life style and acquire new skills? Again, this may need to be simplified to ensure parents answer all three questions. They may need examples and discussion beforehand.

Will parents experience new care needs and require practical help in terms of aids, adaptations or general support during these years? This relates mainly to children who have extensive needs such as severe learning or physical difficulties. It will be important for parents to be advised to be tactful in the use of any labels they might need to use to define their child's needs.

Action 13

1.   Provide simplified questionnaire to parents in advance of meeting.

2.   Help and advise as required

3.   Include or revise information in the light of discussion at meeting, following full consultation with and agreement of parents.

The young person

What information do young people need in order to make informed choices? This can only be established following careful consultation and discussion with the young person. This is likely to be done by the teacher responsible for careers in the school, working closely with the Careers Adviser. They will take their lead from the student and explore options on the young person's behalf, followed by the provision of specific information on the career choices available. This information will probably include a range of:

● suitable courses in FE colleges locally;

● work employment opportunities;

● vocational training schemes.

This information is usually in print but may need to be modified to enable the student full access. Help with discussion and to ensure understanding of the contents of the information may also be needed.

Action 14

1.   Arrange for information to be available at school.

2.   Organise meeting with specialist for student if possible.

3.   Record outcome of discussions and proposals.

What local arrangements exist to provide advocacy and advice if required? The LEA should already have published information on these sources with regard to the statutory assessment procedures. This should be used for the purpose of reference. Alternatively, the voluntary agencies provide a good source.

Action 15

1. Make available within school information on sources for advocacy.
2. Develop contacts with these agencies and include them in discussion and planning where this is acceptable to the student and parents.

How can young people be encouraged to contribute to their own Transition Plan and make positive decisions about the future? This would normally involve extensive preparation by teachers whom the student trusts and can work with. Parents would have also been party to these preliminary discussions and consultations. The main requirement is that the student be able to make informed choices through knowing the options available and those to which he is best suited. Some may not be able to do this on their own, either because of communication difficulties, a lack of understanding of the issues involved, or lack of confidence. This is when they will require strong advocacy, based on insight of their needs and aspirations.

Action 16

1. Explain purpose of Transition Plan.
2. Talk this through so that student understands and can contribute.
3. Provide the fullest information possible.
4. Talk through the 'pros and cons' and determine student's preferences.
5. Provide opportunity for discussion with specialists, e.g. careers adviser.
6. Record discussions and communicate proposals at meeting.
7. Prepare and empower student at meeting.

If young people are living away from home or attending a residential school outside their own LEA, are there special issues relating to the location of services when they leave school which should be discussed in planning? This is especially pertinent to the student returning to the home area, requiring a period of retraining and readjustment to suit his new circumstances. There are issues here for the visually impaired person in particular who may require mobility training, or for the physically disabled whose living accommodation may need to be adapted well in advance. Similarly, individuals with significant medical needs requiring specialist medical help would need to have these agencies alerted beforehand.

Action 17

1.   Make contact with 'home' authorities.

2.   Determine local circumstances and services from these sources.

3.   Alert agencies to requirements through clear specification of student's needs.

4.   Do not pre-empt local decision making; local agencies know their services and circumstances best.

5.   If procedures need to be explained to student and parents, do so or refer them to the most informed party.

What are the young person's hopes and aspirations for the future, and how can these be met? This is the crucial question which can only be answered from extensive knowledge of the young person. Sometimes it is simple enough for teachers to determine the hopes and aspirations, especially if they have been in regular contact with the student and know about his needs, abilities, interests and aptitudes. Some of these may have already been communicated by the student. However, there are instances when teachers, in consultation with parents and other parties, have to determine future choices but this should never be done without firsthand knowledge and teaching of the young person.

Action 18

1.   Meet with young person and/or parents.

2.   Consider profile of attainments, expressed interests, strengths, weaknesses, demonstrable talents.

3.   Determine career aspirations through consultation and discussion with all concerned parties.

4.   Consider match between abilities and interests, and aspirations.

5.   Discuss and agree action.

TRANSITION PLAN FOR (Specimen)

This Plan should be completed at the annual review meeting for a young person in Year 9 and above and should be attached to the Annual Review Report.

Name: Thomas D   Date of Birth: 10.6.81
Address:
Names of Parents/Person Responsible:
School: NC   Year: 9
Date of Current Annual Review Report (attached):
Expected school leaving date:

School perspective

1. Summary of likely curriculum needs up to 18th year and new educational and vocational skills to be developed
(a) Development of numeracy and literacy, including money, budgeting, time and social sight vocabulary.
(b) Development of interpersonal and social skills, e.g. presentation skills, communication, group discussion/collaboration/co-operation, relationships and responsibilities.
(c) Development of life and independence skills, e.g. preparing for work, adult life.
   New skills to be developed:
   Educational Link between work and curriculum experiences, specifically citizenship skills, e.g. development of personal autonomy, creative and independent thinking, decision making.
   Vocational Preparation for training in car maintenance, e.g. timekeeping, practical experience.

2. How will the curriculum help the young person to play a role in the community, make use of leisure and recreational facilities and assume new roles within the family?
(a) Community Care module will provide Tom with opportunities to work with other people the elderly; children, the physically frail or disabled.
(b) Opportunities to extend learning into the community through Link Courses, Citizenship, PSE, Work Studies.
(c) Provision of opportunities to take part in leisure and recreation activities, e.g. skiing, sailing and canoeing, in addition to traditional games and P.E. as available locally.
(d) Develop Tom's awareness of his changing role and responsibilities, including personal, social and financial elements.

People involved
1. Which new professionals need to be involved in planning for transition, e.g. occupational psychologists, the careers service, rehabilitation medicine specialist, occupational and other therapists, representatives from the local college?
(a) Specialist Careers Adviser.
(b) Representatives from specialist courses in local colleges/training agencies (New Horizon).

2. How can they develop close working relationships with colleagues in other agencies to ensure effective and coherent plans for the young person in transition?

(a) Careers Adviser to meet with Tom and his parents to explore suitable post-16 options within the full range available.

(b) Careers Adviser to organise visits/placements once opportunities have been identified and agreed, and to liaise with all parties, including parents.

(c) Representatives to attend relevant meetings at RE school and specify their requirements.

3. Does the young person have any special health or welfare needs which will require planning and support from health and social services now or in the future?

Housing/accommodation is likely to be a requirement at 19+ and will need to be planned for at an early stage.

4. Are assessment arrangements for transition clear, relevant and shared between all agencies concerned?

Information will be available from RE school based on the outcome of Tom's individual experiences. His individual experiences will be evaluated and information integrated within Annual Reviews. He will, however, benefit from assessment by the Training Agency or other relevant body that might become appropriate at the time.

5. How can information best be transferred from children's to adult services to ensure a smooth transitional arrangement?

(a) Pre-transfer meetings and regular liaison.

(b) Full documentation will be sent to receiving agency as soon as transfer identified and agreed.

(c) Use of networking agencies, such as Careers Advisers.

6. Where a young person requires a particular technological aid, do the arrangements for transition include appropriate training and arrangements for securing technological support?

Tom will require continued access to an Archimedes computer or, alternatively, retraining in the use of a personal computer. Relevant software to include word processing with a spellcheck will also be needed.

Family views

1. What do you expect for your child in adult life?

(a) Employment within the car maintenance trade.

(b) Housing/accommodation at 19+.

2. How can you help your child develop personal and social skills, an adult life style and acquire new skills?

(a) Through encouragement, advice and support.

(b) Help to develop his interests and encouragement to attend youth clubs and other groups.

(c) Increasing responsibility to manage his affairs, particularly money.

(d) Help with transition from education to work, e.g. help with applications, interviews, transport.

(e) Support with his training requirements.

3. Will you experience new care needs and require practical help in terms of aids, adaptation or general support during these years?
No.

Young person's views about future educational needs

1. On the job training.
2. Continuing help with literacy and numeracy.

Young person's needs

1. Information requirements:
(a) Post-16 options (leaflets and preferably videos).
(b) Careers software for special needs children.

2. Contact points for advocacy and advice:
(a) RE School
(b) Careers advice (Tel:)

3.   In helping the young person contribute to the Transition Plan, guidance and support have been offered by:
(a) Class teacher, Head of Upper School.

4. Local services, contact names and addresses:
(a) Careers (Tel:)
(b) College (Tel:)

Please list those who contributed to the Transition Plan:

Names   *Position/Relationship*

Signature: Date: Position:

(A copy of the Transition Plan is being circulated to all those who are being sent the Annual Review Report.)

CHAPTER 9

Parents and the Code of Practice

Introduction

The Code of Practice is a comprehensive document, representing an extremely useful source of reference for parents and other parties. It details parental rights and expectations and gives parents and their children a voice on how help should be planned and provided in schools. The Code reinforces key principles and values, some established and enshrined in legislation. Amongst the most important of these are:
- the rights of children and the recognition that their development and welfare is of paramount importance (Children Act 1989);
- the rights of parents to be active and equal partners in supporting children with special educational needs (Warnock Report 1978, 1981 Education Act, 1993 Education Act);
- the responsibilities of parents towards their child's need to receive regular and efficient education (1944 Education Act);
- the responsibilities and accountability of schools, LEAs and other agencies towards children and parents.

Responsibilities of schools towards parents

The Code requires that schools:
- publish their Special Educational Needs Policies (see Chapter 3), which are to be made available to parents and are to be reviewed annually to determine its success or otherwise. These policies must detail the arrangements which operate within the school to identify, assess and provide for children with special educational needs, together with the names of persons who will act as points of contact for parents.
- follow a staged approach to assessing and providing for children with special educational needs, involving parents at each stage. This includes full consultation with the parents and their active involvement from the time their child is identified as having a learning difficulty. The objective is to ensure that parents are able to become equal and active partners, playing a full part in

supporting their child with any educational intervention proposed.
- keep IEPs and other records which are shared with parents and to which they contribute.
- organise regular meetings and reviews with parents at which IEPs can be reviewed in terms of progress achieved, targets set and future action and planning.
- advise parents of their child's needs and progress and guide them through the 'Stages', up to and beyond Stage 5, i.e. after completion of the statutory assessment.
- organise annual reviews for children who are provided with a Statement of Special Educational Needs, ensuring the necessary liaison and consultation on behalf of the LEA.

Responsibilities of schools towards children

The Code requires schools to:
- consult with children and ensure that their feelings and views are represented regarding any planning undertaken on their behalf.
- ensure that children, where they are able, are encouraged to play an active role and to be fully involved, including their attendance at meetings.

Roles and responsibilities of parents

The main legal requirement is that parents ensure that their children receive regular and efficient education (1944 Education Act). An extension of this is the role played by parents in safeguarding the best interests of their child. This is mainly arrived at through advocacy, based on an understanding of children's and parents' rights, including the efficient discharge of the duties and responsibilities undertaken by parents.

The Code makes provision for parents to act as advocates for their child. This is achieved by means of requirements placed on other parties, towards the parents and their children as consumers of the service they receive. The 'duty of care', however, applies to all parties in respect of the assessment procedures, particularly those defined by law, i.e. the statutory multi-professional assessment.

Parents have to be especially careful that they understand and are able to exercise their rights at various stages of their child's statutory assessment. In particular, parents are well advised to understand the processes and systems which apply at the stages preceding statutory assessment. They need to know about the kinds of planning, teaching and documentation required of schools at each stage. This is in order to be able to evaluate these against the Code's recommendations and is particularly important if their child is likely to require statutory assessment. They need to know if schools have indeed exhausted all the options in terms of teaching and provision from within their internal resources. This is because this will have a direct implication on the LEA's response regarding requests for statutory assessment. LEAs are unlikely to agree to undertake statutory assessment unless they are satisfied that exceptional arrangements and resources are required which are beyond the ability of the school to provide. They will also be wanting to evaluate the quality and intensity of the educational intervention, together with the reliability and validity of the documentation and evidence.

Parents' statutory rights Under the 1993 Education Act, parents have the right to:
● request a statutory assessment if they are concerned about their child's learning difficulties. The LEA will need to consider the request and provide the parents with a written decision within six weeks. The LEA will normally have to comply, unless this is considered to be unnecessary.
● refuse to have their child assessed if he is under two years of age; and to make representations against statutory assessment if they consider this to be unnecessary or premature.
● consider their responses to proposals for statutory assessment, whether or not initiated by other parties or at their request. They have a statutory period of 29 days within which to make their views known to the LEA.
● submit their own advice as the 'Parental Advice' to their child's statutory assessment. This will include their assessment of their child as parents, the child's strengths and weaknesses and the help that is needed. Parents may also submit 'Parental Representations', which is advice prepared for them by a professional, friend or adviser working on their behalf. In any event, such advice must be submitted within 29 days, starting from the date of the LEA's proposal letter to carry out the statutory assessment.
● receive a draft copy of the LEA's intended Statement of Special Educational Needs for their child, if one is to be issued within 18 weeks of the start of the statutory assessment procedures. Alternatively, they should receive a 'Note in Lieu' of a statement if one is not to be issued following completion of the statutory assessment, within a time limit of 18 weeks. A Note in Lieu will specify the reasons why a statement is not to be issued, including the consultation available if parents are dissatisfied with such an outcome.
● receive a copy of the final, 'signed' statement within 26 weeks of the date when statutory assessment was started.
● respond and comment on the draft Statement of Special Educational Needs within 15 days of its receipt and either confirm their agreement to it or raise their concerns.
● request a meeting with an LEA officer if they have queries or concerns, again within 15 days. Two further meetings can also be arranged if the matter cannot be resolved but parents need to request these within 15 days of each preceding meeting.
● be guided through the statutory assessment process by a 'Named Officer' of the LEA. This person is to act as their point of contact with the LEA, to answer queries, give advice and generally help parents with the procedure and requirements
● be advised of a 'Named Person' who is independent of the LEA and who can act as a friend and adviser in respect of the statutory assessment.
● state a preference for a school unless this is:
  – incompatible for their child's education
  – incompatible with the education of the majority of the children already

at the school

    – not effective use of resources from the point of view of the LEA.

● appeal to an independent Special Educational Needs Tribunal if they are unable to agree with the LEA's assessment.

● attend annual reviews of their child's Statement.

● be consulted and involved in the preparation of the Transition Plan at the Year 9 Annual Reviews for children aged 14+.

The foregoing is not a complete list but a summary of key issues of which parents need to be aware.

Statutory Time Limits

This diagram sets out the statutory time limits in respect of statutory assessment.

LEA considers whether or not to initiate statutory assessment procedures: *6 weeks. (This usually follows a request from a parent or a recommendation from school or other agency)*

LEA carries out the statutory assessment: *10 weeks. (This is for the seeking and collection of the necessary advice)*

LEA decides whether or not to make a Statement of Special Educational Needs: *2 weeks (LEA's options are to make a Statement or to issue a Note in Lieu)*

LEA finalises the Statement: *8 weeks. (This 8 week period starts from the date the LEA serve the proposed Statement, ending with the date on which the Statement is finalised)*

Exceptions to time limits

The time limit of 26 weeks is waived if the following conditions apply:

    – the child and parents are absent from the area for longer than four weeks;

    – the LEA is aware of exceptional personal circumstances affecting the child or its parents during the assessment period, e.g. illness, family bereavement;

    – the LEA requests advice from a headteacher relating to the request for statutory assessment during a period beginning one week before the school closes for a continuous period of not less than four weeks and ending one week before it is due to re-open;

    – parents are late in their submission of their advice or evidence by six weeks or more dating from the time of the LEA's request to them for such information;

    – the child is not known to the local Health or Social Services Department;

- parents fail to attend appointments with any of the agencies involved in the statutory assessment;
- the parents are unable to agree the draft Statement and seek more than one consultation meeting with an LEA officer to resolve matters;
- the LEA seeks further advice following receipt of all the appendices normally required for the Statement; this may be for the purpose of clarifying issues, seeking further specialist advice or any follow up action the LEA believes to be necessary;
- the LEA requests educational advice during a period beginning one week before the school closes for a continuous period of not less than four weeks and ending one week before it is due to re-open;
- the LEA needs to seek approval to use an independent school and is unable to obtain a decision from the DFE within two weeks.

These exceptions to the statutory time limits apply at various stages of the assessment period. Some apply to the initial six week period when the LEA is considering its response to requests for statutory assessment. Others are specific to the ten week period which follows when the decision is made to proceed with the assessment. The first three exceptions in the above list apply to the former, the rest are more specific to the ten week time limit within which the LEA must make an assessment.

Action for parents

Parents should:
- observe the time limits which apply to all the stages of the statutory assessment procedure.
- request to see IEPs and other records which have been prepared in response to their child's special educational needs. They should ask for clarification of any of the proposals that are unclear to them, and expect to be involved in supporting, monitoring and reviewing their child's progress.
- liaise closely with their child's school and be guided by their advice on what has been done, what is being done and what needs to be done in the future.
- request help, advice and guidance either from the LEA or from the Named Person if they have a query at any stage of the assessment process.
- make their views known to all parties including the LEA, and query any advice or recommendations which appear to diverge from or contradict advice or recommendations offered by others. It will be helpful for parents to seek explanations and justifications from all professionals involved in order to evaluate the rationale and validity of the advice. It is important to avoid confusion and misunderstandings, which can later lead to disagreement or dispute, and thereby obviate a need for formal hearings at Special Educational Needs Tribunals where differences of view will be subject to close scrutiny to determine which is the more valid.
- ensure they are actively involved in all aspects of planning relating to their child's education.

The Roles of Parents in statutory assessments and annual reviews

Parents have a role to play at all stages, including those preceding the decision for statutory assessment to be made. It is important that they involve themselves at Stages 1 to 3 of the Code, i.e. the school based stages when much valuable and preventative work can be done to deal with their child's special needs. They should consult and work closely with their child's teacher and/or Special Educational Needs Co-ordinator, collaborating and supporting initiatives and proposals, activating teaching plans and strategies, and engaging in reviews to determine the progress being made.

Parents do not need to be teachers to make an active contribution to their child's education. There are a number of areas where they, as parents, have a natural and distinct advantage. Parents have the major role with regard to the encouragement and development of self-help, communication, social and life skills which happen everyday in the context of the home. Studies have shown that parents can and do make a difference (see Macbeth, 1989). They can also act as active partners with teachers to help in the teaching and consolidation of a number of skills, e.g. the teaching of reading through 'shared approaches' where the emphasis is on the child and the parents sharing and enjoying the activity. 'Shared reading' constitutes quality family time and involvement for the young child. For the older child in secondary schools, 'paired reading' where child and parent take it in turn to read, has been shown to be effective (see Topping and Wolfendale, 1985; Branston and Provis, 1986; Tizard et al, 1982; Tizard and Hughes, 1984). Similarly, shared writing has been shown to be effective (see Hannavy, 1995).

Parents should therefore be looking at every opportunity to support their child, especially if it is with regard to an activity that they can be confident about sharing and enjoying with their child. However, if this should cause them any worry or anxiety which is likely to be transmitted either consciously or unconsciously, they should avoid becoming involved, leaving the task to teachers and support staff.

Providing advice for statutory assessment

At Stage 4, when the LEA decides to initiate statutory assessment procedures, parents are invited to contribute to the assessment through the provision of written advice. They can prepare this advice themselves or they can seek the help of others, probably a professional adviser, to make written representations on their behalf. The intention is to give them the opportunity to advise the LEA of their child's special educational needs and how these should be met.

Wolfendale (1988) provides some useful guidelines on the parental contribution to assessment and these have been adopted in the Code of Practice. Essentially, they cover parental observations and concerns about both the past and the current situation, including the parent's recommendations for the future.

Parents might wish to consider using the following checklist in the preparation of their advice for submission to the LEA in respect of statutory assessment. This has been adapted from Wolfendale, op.cit., taking account of developments from the Code of Practice.

The past

1. What can you remember about the early years, in terms of your child's development?

2. Were there any problems with the pregnancy, at or after birth?

3. Did anything else of significance happen?

4. When did you start feeling that things were not right? Was your child perhaps slow in sitting up, walking or talking? Was he 'too good' as a baby, 'too placid, never cried'? Did he want/respond to attention? Did he not want to be picked up? Was he a cuddly baby?

5. How did he compare with other children of his age? Did he seem to be behind, perhaps in his speech, his play? Did you worry about his hearing or other aspects of his development? What help did you receive?

The current situation

1. What are your child's strengths, i.e. what is he particularly good at?

2. What are his weaknesses and how could he be helped with these?

3. What are his likes and dislikes? In particular, what should teachers and others be aware of during the school day, to encourage his involvement and minimise the risk of causing him anxiety, distress? Does he have any particular interests that could be used in teaching?

4. How are you helping your child at home? What aspects of this work has been influenced, guided and supported by teachers? Do you feel this is making any difference or would you advise on a change of emphasis in any area?

5. What have been your contributions at meetings in school to review your child's progress? Do you believe anything else should be tried?

6. What is your child's perspective about his current situation?

Special educational needs

1. What do you consider to be your child's most significant needs? Could you list these in priority order? For example, if it is speech, should 'listening' skills be dealt with first, comprehension of simple instructions second and expression/articulation of words third? Do you have any thoughts or advice on what could be stopping your child from making progress?

2. How long have you been aware of your child's special educational needs? What has been done about these?

3. How is your child coping/dealing with his learning difficulties? Does he feel he is getting the right/adequate support? What other help would he like/benefit from?

The future: both immediate and long term

1. What should happen now? At home, at school? What is needed immediately?

2. What are your main worries/concerns?

3. What is the best way of helping? Has this been tried before and should anything be done differently this time?

4. Who is the best person to help and how frequently should the help be provided?

5. How is your child's progress going to be monitored, i.e. how would you/your child's teacher know that he is making the intended progress?

6. How long would you be waiting between progress meetings/reviews?

7. Is the help that you are looking for immediately available in your child's school? Describe the arrangements you would wish for your child. What is his perspective/view about the future?

A photocopiable copy of the above checklist is included in Appendix 6.

Parents' advice for annual reviews

Parents have a right to contribute advice, both written and verbal, in respect of annual reviews. Written advice is required, by law, of schools and the LEA and is an option for parents of which they should take advantage.

In preparing their advice, parents may find the following helpful. They may also wish to refer to the 'Agenda for Parents at Annual Reviews' which is covered in Chapter 7 of this book.

Special educational needs: the past

1. What does the Statement say about their child's special educational needs? Is this still accurate?

2. How have the special educational needs in the Statement been addressed? What has worked? What has not worked so well? What remains to be done and how?

3. Observations on the teaching arrangements/strategies. What has been effective/not so effective and how should changes/improvements be made?

4. In relation to targets set, how many have been achieved? Which are proving hard to deal with and what else is required? Is there evidence of progress, if not, why not?

The present and future

1. What are the priorities for the coming year? What is the best way of achieving these, in the light of past experience?

2. What help would the child/the parents/the school need?

3. Are there concerns about the curriculum? What are they? How could these be addressed and what are the legal constraints, e.g. specific curricular requirements at Key Stages such as the need for a modern foreign language at secondary stage.

4. What are the contingency arrangements in the event of proposals and plans needing to be dropped/changed? What should be the process in terms of consultation, their involvement? This is particularly important, especially if the parents themselves decide to initiate changes.

The child's perspective

1. How does the child feel about the past year? What achievements has he

made and what are the challenges that he wants to undertake?

2. What are his priorities and how do these fit in with his own plans/aspirations for the future?

3. Is he comfortable with all the arrangements, e.g. staff, resources, physical arrangements, pace of learning, expectations, level of support?

4. How does he view himself in comparison with his peers? What help does he need?

A version of the above checklist is also included in Appendix 7.

What can parents expect of their LEAs?

Parents can expect their LEAs to:

- provide information relating to the statutory assessment procedures. This should be made available in a number of languages in order to be accessible to parents to whom English is a second language. LEAs are also obliged to provide interpreters when this is needed.
- provide guidance during and throughout the statutory assessment procedures and to keep the parents informed as to progress, when required to do so. This is normally the responsibility of the Named Officer.
- deal with parents' requests and queries in respect of statutory assessment promptly and effectively, within the specified time limit which applies at each stage of the process.

Parents as education partners?

The Code makes it clear that parents should be seen as partners in the education of their child. They have a wealth of firsthand experience and expertise which ought to be tapped by teachers and others, if a thorough understanding of the whole child and his circumstances is to be achieved. Parents can provide information relating to the level and degree of support they can make available at home, and the resource that they represent to teachers and the child should not be underestimated.

Education is a twenty-four hour, life long process and if this view is accepted it becomes clear that parents are the active educators for the majority of the time each day, albeit not always necessarily working on the same curricula. Research suggests that when these do coincide with the school's priorities, there are effective and beneficial outcomes all round; examples being parental partnership in shared reading schemes, portage.

Special Educational Needs Tribunals

There will be occasions when, in spite of the best endeavours, parents and their LEAs are unable to agree on the best course of action. This is why Special Educational Needs Tribunals have come into being. The tribunal is an independent body, led by a legally qualified chairman, set up under the 1993 Education Act to determine appeals by parents against LEA decisions on assessments and statements. It replaces the appeal committees that existed before implementation of the 1993 Act. These were staffed by teams of county councillors and could only make recommendations to the LEA which could choose to ignore them, leaving appeal to the Secretary of State as the only recourse open to parents. Their impartiality was also questioned as councillors were perceived as protective of the LEA's interests.

The tribunals on the other hand, make decisions which are binding on both parties to the appeal. They should bring consistency, fairness and expertise to appeals, but could become threatening and legalistic.

Parents can appeal to the tribunal if they are unhappy with their LEA's decision:

- not to assess their child, following a request from them;
- not to issue a statement on completion of the statutory assessment;
- to cease to maintain an existing statement.

If a statement is made or an existing statement is amended, they can also appeal against:

- the LEA's description in Part II of the child's special educational needs;
- the special education provision described in Part III;
- the school named in Part IV, or that none has been named.

Parents have to appeal within two months of receiving the LEA decision, using a signed Notice of Appeal form. If the tribunal decides that the appeal is within its remit, the following timetable applies. The whole process, between parents lodging an appeal and the tribunal hearing, is not expected to take longer than four or five months.

Special Educational Needs Tribunal: Timetable

1. Parents appeal within two months of receiving LEA decision.

2. Tribunal sends 'Appeal Notice' to LEA within 10 working days.

3. LEA has to confirm its response within 20 working days, i.e. whether or not to resist the appeal and on what grounds.

---

4. Tribunal sends LEA's response to parents, this being at the time of receipt.

5. Parents may comment on LEA's response within 15 working days.

6. Tribunal sends forms to LEA and parents, requesting details of how they are to be represented at the hearing. Forms required to be returned within 30 working days.

---

7. Parties notified of date, time and place of hearing at least 10 working days beforehand.

8. Written notification of tribunal decision within 10 working days of hearing.

Issues outside the remit of tribunals

Special Educational Needs Tribunals have no power to deal with parental complaints about:

- the way a school is providing for a child's needs, or failing to do so;
- the length of time the LEA takes to assess or provide a statement for a child;
- the way in which the LEA describes the child's non-educational needs in Part V and the manner in which it intends to provide for them;
- the way in which the LEA conducts the assessment and how it arranges the help specified in the statement.

In these cases, parents have recourse to one of the following, each of which has varying powers:

- the governing body of the school;
- the LEA;
- the local Member of Parliament;
- the Secretary of State;
- the Local Government Ombudsman;

or they can seek a judicial review through the High Court. Who the parents approach will depend on the nature of their complaint and the channel most appropriate in terms of powers of jurisdiction.

Costs

Tribunals will not normally award costs except in exceptional circumstances, if, in its view, either party is acting frivolously, vexatiously or unreasonably. Legal aid is not available for tribunals but can be available to the child in respect of judicial review, though some of the initial legal costs are not covered.

SEN Tribunals: the first six months

Tribunals started to operate in September 1994. By May 1995 some 500 appeals had been received and about 50 had been heard and disposed of, with one decision due to be challenged in the High Court. This concerns the placement of a 13 year old boy in a comprehensive school in Westminster. The tribunal ruled that the school is able to meet his needs but directed the LEA to rewrite the statement. The parents are appealing, believing the school to be inappropriate.

Half the number of appeals have been in respect of children with specific learning difficulties and the reasons for these are:

- against the LEA's decision to make a statement (30 per cent)
- against the contents of the statement (25 per cent)
- against refusal to assess (20 per cent)
- against school named in the statement (18 per cent).

Appeals are being received at the rate of around 30 a week. If this were to continue, it would not be long before the system came to a standstill. There is already a considerable backlog of some 450 cases and at the current pace of work it may be predicted that within a year another 100 cases would have been heard, with a total of 1,960 appeals outstanding. This may sound pessimistic and alarmist, but unless the take up shows some sign of slowing down, the system is likely to clog up, killing off all hopes of speedy resolution to disputes as intended by the Government.

The costs are also likely to be prohibitive to all parties, including tribunal staff, LEAs and parents. Early indications show a trend towards legal representation at tribunals. This is in spite of previous efforts by the DFE to discourage LEAs from bringing lawyers to tribunals if the parents are not legally represented. Given the high costs of legal representation and the time needed to be spent by LEA staff dealing with tribunal cases, it is not surprising that concerns have been voiced that tribunals would inexorably add to the cost of special educational needs provision (Wright, 1994). Even more worrying would be the need to find extra money to fund tribunal decisions which go against the LEA as this inevitably means more being spent on some and considerably less on others. Therefore, the intention of the DFE for tribunals to be 'cost neutral' will soon prove to have been a dream which could not stand up to the harsh reality that arbitration does not necessarily restrain demand. One such dream that must surely now be a nightmare is how to have cases heard within six months of the appeal notice being filed.

As far as parents are concerned there is the problem of deciding whether or not to be represented. Many may consider this to be essential if they are to stand a good chance of securing the provision they wish for their child. Going to a tribunal is not a decision that they would have taken lightly and it is not inconceivable that they may wish to have the support of lawyers in order to challenge the LEA. The latter, whether legally represented or not, must appear to be formidable even to the most able and talented of parents, on the grounds of educational experience and expertise, notwithstanding the resources the LEA is able to draw on. Time will tell how many parents resist the urge for legal representation, especially those who can afford it.

On a more positive note, Aldridge, who is the President of the SEN Tribunal, believes that cases are being heard promptly, within a reasonably informal atmosphere (Aldridge, 1995). He also confirms that the tribunals are likely to favour the approach which promotes the child's best interest, as opposed to sitting in judgement on the LEA's decision making process. They will be looking at all the evidence on which the LEA's original decision is based, including new information which is considered relevant to the child's needs.

Some final comments

The Code of Practice has been welcomed in many quarters as representing a significant milestone in furthering the cause of children with special educational needs. It provides, as it sets out to do, clear, detailed and practical guidance relating to how children are to be supported in schools, including the procedures, processes and systems to be followed, thereby building in efficiencies and accountabilities. The Code in itself provides a structure for all

schools and if followed has the potential to lead to the following benefits:
- planned, active and systematic consultation and involvement of children and their parents on how they are helped with their education;
- a clearer appreciation of children's entitlement and parental rights and expectations;
- detailed guidance for all parties relating to the requirements of the 1993 Education Act;
- minimum requirements from all schools on policies, procedures and practices with regard to children with special educational needs, particularly in respect of the staged approach to assessment, the preparation of IEPs and the expectations from Annual Review especially at Year 9;
- public reporting of a school's successes or otherwise relating to the implementation of their special educational needs policies;
- increased efficiencies and accountabilities, particularly from LEA staff with regard to statutory assessment and annual reviews.

However, as with other legislative initiatives, the Code has its critics. Amongst the concerns raised are:
- the increased bureaucracy that may result from its implementation, especially in the absence of increased resources;
- the additional workload to teachers, and SEN Co-ordinators in particular, due to the requirement to maintain Special Educational Needs Registers, in addition to other documentation and evidence expected as a matter of routine;
- time constraints, made worse through the increased requirements for formal consultation between teachers, parents and other interested parties;
- raised expectations of some parties and the inabilities of others to work within limited, finite resources;
- the use of bureaucratic procedures to chase and add to inadequate resources;
- an increase in confrontation, disputes and appeals, using any loopholes which the Code could be offering inadvertently.

The DFE believes that implementation of the Code should be cost neutral, as they expect that schools should already be following the model of practice that it offers, providing a structured approach to how children with special needs are supported in their learning. However, audits carried out in Cambridge LEA suggest the following breakdowns, with regard to additional workloads generated at each stage of the Code, per child.

Stage	Teacher Time
Stage 1	4.9 hours
Stage 2	5.2 hours
Stage 3	6.0 hours
Stage 4	2.0 hours
Stage 5	7.0 hours

Johnson (1995) quantifies the above as requiring 878 hours, i.e. 0.9 of a whole teacher equivalent, in an 11–16 comprehensive school of 1,000 children. This is based on an estimate derived from audits carried out in Kent and Lambeth LEAs that the following percentages of children will require help at each of the stages.

Stage	Percentage
Stage 1	7%
Stage 2	4%
Stage 3	5%
Stages 4 & 5	2%

It is therefore no wonder that there are concerns in schools and LEAs on how to fund the requirements which are likely to arise. Inevitably, there will be more demand for resources which are already short (Lunt and Evans, 1994). Linked with this will be an increased likelihood of discontent and conflict paving the way for appeals. Education could then become the happy hunting ground for lawyers, which has been predicted for some time (*Times Educational Supplement*, 25 February, 1994).

This was not what the Code intended. However, should it fail to influence practice at the 'grass roots', it may well join with other legislation now seen as rhetoric such as those dealing with children's rights (see Gersch et al, 1993). Currently, there is the reality in education and elsewhere of too many chasing too few resources. Inevitably, there are gainers and losers. The danger is though, that the more powerful and articulate will stand to gain at the expense of the more vulnerable and needy. If the Code succeeds in achieving consistency and a degree of uniformity in school practices for the majority of children with special educational needs, then it should be judged a success. How it will fare however, only time will tell.

Appendix 1

SPECIAL EDUCATIONAL NEEDS (SEN) REGISTER

SCHOOL:

DATE:

YEAR GROUP:

MAINTAINED BY:

Name	D.o.B.	Date notified	Stage	SPECIAL EDUCATIONAL NEEDS (or nature of concern)	ACTION (by whom)	MEETING (M) OR REVIEW (R) with parents + dates

Appendix 2

How to formulate and write an Special Educational Needs Policy

1. Agree school's mission statement or equivalent at governors' meeting.
2. Use the mission statement to frame Special Educational Needs Policy.
3. Define Special Needs Policy in the context of:
    - the school's ethos
    - the school's needs and objectives
    - the school's aspirations for all children
    - the governing body's values and principles
    - the children's entitlement
    - parents' rights and expectations.

4. Detail in priority order:
    - the principal objectives of the Special Educational Needs Policy
    - the arrangements to operate within school to support the Policy and in particular, the financial and human resource arrangements.

5. Provide the names of key staff, including that of the Special Educational Needs Co-ordinator and of the Responsible Person, who are to act as links with parents and outside agencies.

6. Describe how:
    - children's learning difficulties are to be identified
    - children are to be helped
    - children's progress is to be reviewed and evaluated.

7. Include information relating to:
    - any specialism available from school staff
    - expertise that can be called or bought in
    - special facilities, resources
    - means of enabling access to these facilities.

8. Include details of the procedures and processes to be followed in the event of:
    - a query
    - a complaint.

9. Describe the consultation and partnership arrangements with:
    - parents and other parties
    - statutory agencies.

10. Include information on how success in achieving the objectives of the Policy is to be evaluated and its form and frequency of reporting.

11. Include a summary of the special educational needs policy in the school prospectus.

Appendix 3(i)

Individual Education Plan (Example)

(This Appendix contains examples of other formats of Individual Education Plans, see Chapter 4)

Name: Date of Birth: Class: Date completed:

Long term goal:

Date	Targets	Teaching Arrangements	Success Criteria	Date Start	Date Finish

Appendix 3(ii)

Individual Education Plan (Example)

Name: Date of Birth: Class: Date completed:

Date	Target	Environmental Change	New Skills	Reinforcement	Success Criteria

Appendix 3 (iii)

Individual Education Plan (Behaviour)

Name: Gary   Date of Birth: 3.4.83   NC Year: 7

Priority:
To reduce incidents of verbal aggression, specifically shouting in the classroom

Behaviour to be addressed: Shouting in class.
Timescale: 10 weeks (dates)
Review Date:

Baseline level:
* Shouting occurs on average five to six times a day.

Objectives:
Andrew will sit near to his teacher and will:

1. Verbalise his needs, comments and responses to questions without shouting.
2. Seek eye contact, raise his hand and wait to be asked to speak at least once a day, without needing to shout out.
3. Write down some of his requests for his teacher to read and respond to.
4. Communicate his feelings to his teacher by using a card, blue for worried, red for angry and green for impatience/need for attention.

Appendix 3(iv)

Individual Education Plan (Behaviour)

Teaching strategy:

1.1 Agree with Andrew how he should be communicating to his teacher in order to gain the best response.

1.2 Spend one minute at the beginning of each lesson to remind Andrew of agreed communication strategy in class.

1.3 Agree with Andrew that teacher will show a photograph of herself asking him to be quiet and will not respond if/when he shouts.

2.1 Ask Andrew to look at teacher, raise his hand and wait for teacher to respond. Teacher will indicate yes/no either verbally or through gesture, e.g. nodding.

2.2 Allocate 2–3 minutes at the beginning of each lesson for Andrew to ask teacher any questions/queries he might have.

2.3 Allocate 2–3 minutes weekly to practise question/answer exercise, consolidating this.

2.4 Teach/play waiting games, using a timer.

Week 1:

Day 1 – Wait 1 minute before speaking.

Day 2 – Wait 1.5 minutes,etc

3.1 Teacher to write in spelling book requests Andrew is likely to make, including a drawing to illustrate.

3.2 Teacher to add words as and when necessary.

3.3 Andrew to learn word spelling and to write his request to teacher.

4.1 Teach and ensure Andrew knows the colours, red, blue and green.

4.2 Practise colour: response games, using cards, e.g. matching colours to pictures, red = angry face, green = help, etc.

Success criteria:

1 Shouting will reduce to 3/4 times a day in week 1

2/3 times a day in week 2, etc.

0 times a day by week 10.

Appendix 3(v)

Individual Education Plan (Behaviour)

Monitoring arrangements:

Success Chart to be kept by teacher and Andrew. Full completion leads to agreed reward.

* Record book to be maintained by teacher, with support from SNA.
* Teacher/parent communication daily in home/school record book.
* Daily review sessions with Andrew and SNA (2–3 minutes).
* Weekly review sessions with Andrew and SNA (10 minutes) to include feedback and advice/teaching.
* Termly review with SENCO and parents (20 minutes).

Provision:

   * Support from SNA.

Role of SNA:

Help: for practice sessions
     in the classroom
for teacher when she is working with Andrew to supervise class, etc.

Outcomes:

Appendix 4

(This Appendix is a Checklist of questions to ask at Stage 2 of the Code of Practice, see Chapter 5)

Stage 2: Checklist

Name: **Date of Birth:**   **Year:**

Learning difficulties

What is now known about the child's learning difficulty?

What methods have been tried and which ones have been more successful?

Are there areas where practice could be improved?

Priority

What is the priority area for attention and remediation?

Does this need to be broken down into sub-areas so that manageable objectives can be set?

Teaching strategy

Why did children not respond to the arrangements made at Stage 1?

Where are adjustments/revisions required?

Should the focus be more on the child's learning style or greater differentiation of the curriculum?

Should teaching be in even smaller steps?

Staffing arrangements

What staffing arrangements need to be made to provide the child with the help that he or she needs?

How will this help be secured, organised, monitored and evaluated?

Signed   **Designator (e.g. SENCo) Date**

Appendix 5

(This Appendix is a Checklist of questions to ask at Stage 3 of the Code of Practice, see Chapter 5)

Stage 3: Checklist

Nature of learning difficulty

Are the child's needs so complex as to require significantly more help and a different type of approach to that provided earlier?

Teaching and assessment

Have the teaching interventions been systematically planned and given sufficient time to work?

Have these been based on concrete evidence of assessment? Give details.

Which areas of the child's functioning seem to be more resistant to change?

Priorities for action and performance indicators

What are the priority areas to address?

What would serve as useful indicators to monitor and evaluate progress?

Concensus on learning difficulty

What is the consensus of opinion on the child's learning difficulty?

Does the child/parent/teacher/support staff feel that: (a) appropriate and (b) sufficient help has been given?

Consultation with teachers

Have all teachers been consulted? (It is essential in secondary schools to consult with teachers and establish their views. In which areas do they feel the child is doing well, which strategies are more likely to bear fruit?)

Consultation with parents

How do parents feel about the whole process?

Do they believe that they have been adequately consulted/involved?

Consultation with the child

How does the child feel?

Does the child understand and is he or she committed to the plan?

Does the child consider it realistic and what level of responsibility is he or she prepared/able to accept?

Standards setting and contingency planning

Have expectations and standards been clearly specified? Give details.

Which support structures are required to facilitate achievement of these? What are they?

What are the contingency arrangements to deal with problems, failures and unplanned events?

Appendix 6

(Parents might use this Checklist when preparing advice for submission to the LEA in respect of statutory assessment)

Parents advice to statutory assessment: checklist

The past

1. What can you remember about the early years, in terms of your child's development?
2. Were there any problems with the pregnancy, at or after birth?
3. Did anything else of significance happen?
4. When did you start feeling that things were not right? Was your child perhaps slow in sitting up, walking or talking? Was he 'too good' as a baby, 'too placid, never cried'? Did he want/respond to attention? Did he not want to be picked up? Was he a cuddly baby?
5. How did he compare with other children of his age? Did he seem to be behind, perhaps in his speech, his play? Did you worry about his hearing or other aspects of his development? What help did you receive?

The current situation

1. What are your child's strengths, i.e. what is he particularly good at?
2. What are his weaknesses and how could he be helped with these?
3. What are his likes and dislikes? In particular, what should teachers and others be aware of during the school day, to encourage his involvement and minimise the risk of causing him anxiety, distress? Does he have any particular interests that could be used in teaching?
4. How are you helping your child at home? What aspects of this work has been influenced, guided and supported by teachers? Do you feel this is making any difference or would you advise on a change of emphasis in any area?
5. What have been your contributions at meetings in school to review your child's progress? Do you believe anything else should be tried?
6. What is your child's perspective about his current situation?

Special educational needs

1. What do you consider to be your child's most significant needs? Could you list these in priority order? For example, if it is speech, should 'listening' skills be dealt with first, comprehension of simple instructions second and expression/articulation of words third? Do you have any thoughts or advice on what could be stopping your child from making progress?
2. How long have you been aware of your child's special educational needs? What has been done about these?
3. How is your child coping/dealing with his learning difficulties? Does he feel he is getting the right/adequate support? What other help would he like/benefit from?

The future: both immediate and long term

1. What should happen now? At home, at school? What is needed immediately?
2. What are your main worries/concerns?
3. What is the best way of helping? Has this been tried before and should anything be done differently this time?
4. Who is the best person to help and how frequently should the help be provided?
5. How is your child's progress going to be monitored, i.e. how would you/your child's teacher know that he is making the intended progress?
6. How long would you be waiting between progress meetings/reviews?
7. Is the help that you are looking for immediately available in your child's school? Describe the arrangements you would wish for your child. What is his perspective/view about the future?

Appendix 7

(Parents might use this Checklist when preparing advice for Annual Reviews)
Parents' advice to annual review: checklist

Special educational needs: the past
1. What does the Statement say about their child's special educational needs? Is this still accurate?
2. How have the special educational needs in the Statement been addressed? What has worked? What has not worked so well? What remains to be done and how?
3. Observations on the teaching arrangements/strategies. What has been effective/not so effective and how should changes/improvements be made?
4. In relation to targets set, how many have been achieved? Which are proving hard to deal with and what else is required? Is there evidence of progress, if not, why not?

The present and the future
1. What are the priorities for the coming year? What is the best way of achieving these, in the light of past experience?
2. What help would the child/the parents/the school need?
3. Are there concerns about the curriculum? What are they? How could these be addressed and what are the legal constraints, e.g. specific curricular requirements at key stages such as the need for a modern foreign language at secondary stage.
4. What are the contingency arrangements in the event of proposals and plans needing to be dropped/changed? What should be the process in terms of consultation and their involvement? This is particularly important, especially if the parents themselves decide to initiate changes.

The child's perspective
1. How does the child feel about the past year? What achievements has he made and what are the challenges that he wants to undertake?
2. What are his priorities and how do these fit in with his own plans/aspirations for the future?
3. Is he comfortable with all the arrangements, e.g. staff, resources, physical arrangements, pace of learning, expectations, level of support?
4. How does he view himself in comparison with his peers? What help does he need?

Appendix 8

Action list for professional advisers at Transition Plan meetings

1. Come to the meeting prepared, i.e:

   Read the Statement

   Bring the file

   Make notes of the chronology of significant events

2. If time allows, produce a summary of the key issues in advance. This helps to focus the discussion.

3. Be clear about own role and do not make promises which cannot be kept.

4. Stick to areas of expertise. Do not stray into others.

5. Keep the focus on *needs*, not *provision*.

6. Make use of Records of Achievement, with consent.

7. Make notes at Transition Plan meeting to enable accuracy of record to be checked.

8. Ensure information is put together in a positive manner and presents young person in a positive light.

9. If you are responsible for producing the Transition Plan, make sure all parties are agreed on the records, especially the action.

Role of professional advisers: Issues to be addressed at the Transition Plan meeting

- Curriculum for the next two years and how this links into longer term plans?
- Priorities for action:

   within *two* years

   at 16+

   Who does what, how, with what and by when?
- The young person's perspective
- The family's perspective
- Short, medium and long term plans for:

   the School

   others
- Essential links and the transition arrangements
- Legal Requirements: Children Act 1989; Disabled Person's Act 1986; The National Health Service and Community Care Act (1990).

Glossary

Annual Review
A statutory meeting convened to review a child's statement of special educational needs. This considers the requirements of the statement, reviews the steps taken to help the child and sets targets in terms of future teaching plans and action.

Appendix
This refers to the written submission of parents or the report of professional advisers in relation to a child's statutory assessment.

Parents are invited to submit their advice or representation.

Appendices are also routinely sought from teachers (Appendix D), doctors (Appendix E), Educational Psychologists (Appendix F) and social workers (Appendix G).

Appendix A
This constitutes the Parental Representation, see Parental Representation below.

Appendix B
This represents the Parental evidence submitted by the child's parents in connection with the statutory assessment.

Appendix C
This constitutes the parental advice, written by or on behalf of parents to represent their views about their child's special educational needs.

Centile
This refers to the position achieved by a child in comparison with his peers. For example, a child who is at the 2nd centile in relation to his height is in the bottom 2% for his age group as far as height is concerned. The same applies to reading or spelling, except that this would refer to his performance on a specific test, as compared with the performance of others in his age group.

Code of Practice
A guide to schools, Local Education Authorities (LEAs), Health and Social Services Departments about the help they can give to children with special educational needs (SEN). Schools and LEAs must have regard to the Code in their dealings with children with special needs.

Draft Statement of Special Educational Needs
The LEA's proposed Statement of Special Educational Needs. It is unsigned and undated but contains all the advice submitted during the assessment procedure. The draft is only a proposal and a consultation document and has no legal validity. It cannot be appealed against, until it is finalised, i.e. until after it is signed and dated by a duly authorised officer of the LEA.

Individual Education Plan (IEP)
A plan prepared by teachers in consultation with parents and others, to help children with special educational needs. This should set out the nature of the learning difficulty, the action required and the strategies to be used, including the staffing arrangements to be made.

Learning Difficulties
A child has a learning difficulty if he or she finds it much harder to learn than most children of the same age.

Local Education Authority (LEA)
Local Government body responsible for providing education and for carrying out statutory assessments and maintaining Statements.

Named Officer
An officer of the LEA who deals with statutory assessments and who acts as the point of contact for parents.

Named Person
A person who is independent of the LEA and who provides information and advice to parents about the assessment procedures. A named person can be a friend, relative or a member of a voluntary organisation.

Note in Lieu of Statement
A note issued by the LEA on completion of the statutory assessment. This is provided instead of a Statement and should normally set out the reasons why a Statement has not been issued.

Parent	The word 'Parent' in this book refers to any adult who exercises parental responsibility for the child, whether a natural parent or not or who has care of the child. This adopts the definition as laid down in the Children Act 1989 to which the reader is referred for more details.
Parental Representation	This is advice prepared by a professional adviser, on behalf of parents in respect of the statutory assessment of their child's special educational needs.
Responsible Person	A Governor, acting on behalf of the Governing Body, or Headteacher, who undertakes responsibility for discharging the school's special educational needs policy. This person must be kept informed about children's special educational needs and will ensure that teachers are aware of children who have been issued with a Statement of Special Educational Needs and their responsibilities towards them.
SEN Co-ordinator	A teacher who has responsibility for co-ordinating special needs within their school.
Special Educational Needs (SEN)	A child has special educational needs if he or she has learning difficulties calling for special educational provision.
Special Educational Provision	The special help given to children with special educational needs.
Special Educational Needs Tribunal	An independent body that hears appeals against decisions made by LEAs. It has a legally qualified chairman and two other 'lay' members, one with experience in the special needs field. Its decisions are binding on parties involved in the appeal.
Statement of Special Educational Needs	A legal document which sets out a child's needs and the extra help to be provided. This is in six parts.

- Part 1 is the introduction and lists biographical and other details, e.g. religion, home address, names of parents/guardians.
- Part 2 details the special educational needs as identified from the statutory assessment.
- Part 3 describes the Special Educational Provision to be made, including the teaching objectives and arrangements necessary to provide for the child's special needs.
- Part 4 names the type of school or other educational placement to be made.
- Part 5 describes any non-educational needs the child has, e.g. he may be asthmatic or epileptic or may require to be looked after by the Social Services, i.e. his needs are not strictly educational and are to be provided by other than the LEA.
- Part 6 specifies the non-educational provision to meet the child's non-educational needs, e.g. physiotherapy, speech therapy or help from the Social Services.

With the Statement, the Appendices which are the reports provided by contributors to the assessment, will be attached.

Statutory Assessment	A very detailed examination of a child's special educational needs, undertaken by the LEA and carried out by a variety of professionals, including teachers, doctors and educational psychologists.
Talking Pendown	A voice synthesizer embedded in a word processor to help children with the development of their literacy skills. The computer 'talks' to the child, giving him instant feedback on the words that he is working with. (See Archimedes Talking Pendown: Software and Guide Book, published by Longman Logotron, 1993.)
Transition Plan	A plan drawn up at the first annual review after a child's fourteenth birthday. It sets out the steps and action needed to help the young person move from school to adult life.

Useful addresses

Action for Sick Children, Argyle House, 29-31 Euston Road, London NW1 2SD.

Advisory Centre for Education, 18 Aberdeen Studios, 22 Highbury Grove, London N5 2EA.

AFASIC – Overcoming Speech Impairments, 347 Central Market, Smithfield, London EC1A 9NH.

Association for Brain Damaged Children, 47 Northumberland Road, Coventry CV1 3AP.

Association for Spina Bifida and Hydrocephalus, Ashbah House, 42 Park Road, Peterborough PE1 2UQ.

British Diabetic Association, 10 Queen Anne Street, London W1M 0BD.

British Dyslexia Association, 98 London Road, Reading RG1 5AU.

British Epilepsy Association, Anstey House, 40 Hanover Square, Leeds LS3 1BE.

British Sports Association for the Disabled, Hayward House, Barnard Crescent, Aylesbury, Bucks HP21 0PG.

Brittle Bone Society, Ward 8, Strathmartine Hospital, Strathmartine, Dundee DD3 0PG.

Centre for Studies on Integration in Education, 4th Floor, 415 Edgware Road, London NW2 6NB.

The Children's Society, Edward Rudolph House, Margery Street, London WC1X 0JL.

Contact-A-Family, 170 Tottenham Court Road, London W1P 0HA.

Council for Disabled Children, c/o National Children's Bureau, 8 Wakley Street, London EC1V 7QE.

Cystic Fibrosis Research Trust, Alexandra House, 5 Blyth Road, Bromley, Kent BR1 3RS.

DIAL UK, 117 High Street, Clay Cross, Derbyshire. (Nationwide telephone information and advice services).

Disability Alliance, ERA, 1st Floor East, Universal House, 88-94 Wentworth Street, London E1 7SA.

Disabled Living Foundation, 380–384 Harrow Road, London W9 2HU.

Down's Syndrome Association, 155 Mitcham Road, London SW17 9PG.

Family Fund, Joseph Rowntree Memorial Trust, PO Box 50, York YO1 1UY.

Friedreich's Ataxia Group, The Common, Cranleigh, Surrey GU8 8SB.

Greater London Association for Disabled People, 336 Brixton Road, London SW9 7AA.

Haemophilia Society, 123 Westminster Bridge Road, London SE1 7HR.

Handicapped Adventure Playground Association, Fulham Palace, Bishops Avenue, London SW6 6EA.

Huntington's Disease Association, 108 Battersea High Street, London SW11 3HP.

Hyperactive Children's Support Group, 71 Whyke Lane, Chichester, Sussex PO19 2LD.

I CAN, Barbican City Gate, 1-3 Dufferin Street, London EC1Y 8NA.

IN TOUCH, 10 Norman Road, Sale, Cheshire M33 3DF. (Information and contacts for rare handicapping conditions.)

IPSEA, 22 Warren Hill Road, Woodbridge, Suffolk IP12 4DU.

KIDS, 80 Waynflete Square, London W10 6UD.

Leukaemia Care Society, PO Box 82, Exeter, Devon EX2 5DP.

MENCAP (Royal Society for Mentally Handicapped Children and Adults), 117-123 Golden Lane, London EC1Y 0RT.

MIND (National Association for Mental Health), 22 Harley Street, London W1N

Motability, Gate House, West Gate, The High, Harlow, Essex CM10 1HR. 01279 635666.

Muscular Dystrophy Group of Great Britain, 7-11 Prescott Place, London SW4 6BS.

National Association for the Education of Sick Children, Open School, 18 Victoria Park Square, London E2 9PF.

National Association of Special Educational Needs (NASEN), Nasen House, 4-5 Amber Business Village, Amber Close, Amington, Tamworth, Staffs B77 4RP.

National Autistic Society, 276 Willesden Lane, London NW2 5RB.

National Deaf Children's Society, 45 Hereford Road, London W2 5AH.

National Eczema Society, 4 Tavistock Place, London WC1H 9RA.

National Federation of the Blind of the UK, Unity House, Smyth Street, Westgate, Wakefield, West Yorkshire WF1 1ER.

National Library for the Handicapped Child, Ash Court, Rose Street, Wokingham, Berks RG11 1XS.

National Physically Handicapped and Able Bodied, Padholme Road East, Peterborough PE1 5UL.

National Portage Association, 4 Clifton Road, Winchester, Hants. (Work with parents of young handicapped children.)

National Rathbone Society, 1st Floor, Princess House, 105-107 Princess Street, Manchester M1 6DD.

National Toy Libraries Association, 68 Churchway, London NW1 1LT.

NETWORK, 16 Princeton Street, London WC1R 4BB.

NETWORK 81, 1-7 Woodfield Terrace, Chapel Hill, Stansted, Essex CM24 8AJ.

Parents In Partnership, Unit 2, Ground Floor, 70 South Lambert Road, London SW8 1RL.

Pre-school Playgroup Association, 61-63 Kings Cross Road, London WC1X 9LL.

Royal Association for Disability and Rehabilitation, 12 City Forum, 250 City Road, London EC1V 8AF.

Royal National Institute for the Blind, 224 Great Portland Street, London W1N 6AA.

Royal National Institute for the Deaf, 105 Gower Street, London WC1E 6AH.

SCOPE, (formerly known as The Spastics Society), 12 Park Crescent, London W1N 4EQ.

SENSE, 11-13 Clifton Terrace, Finsbury Park, London N4 3SR.

Sickle Cell Society, 54 Station Road, London NW10 4UA.

SKILL (formerly the National Bureau for Handicapped Students), 336 Brixton Road, London SW9 7AA.

Special Education Consortium, c/o Council for Disabled Children, 8 Wakley Street, London EC1V 7QE.

Spinal Injuries Association, Newpoint House, 76 St James Lane, London N10 3DF.

Stroke Association, CHSA House, Whitecross Street, London EC1Y 8JJ.

Tuberous Sclerosis Association of Great Britain, Martell Mount, Holywell Road, Malvern, Wells, Worcestershire WR14 4LF.

Young Minds, 22a Boston Place, London NW1 6ER.

(List reproduced from DFE: Special Educational Needs: A Guide for Parents, May 1994.)

Further reading and references

HMSO/DFE publications

Audit Commission/HMI (1992a), *Getting in on the Act: A Management Handbook for Schools and LEAs*. HMSO.
Audit Commission/HMI (1992b), *Getting the Act Together*. HMSO.
The Children Act 1989. HMSO.
Children and Young People (1978), (The Warnock Report). Department of Education and Science (DES).
Circular 11/90, Staffing for pupils with special educational needs guidance. DFE.
Code of Practice on the identification and assessment of special educational needs 1994. DFE and Welsh Office.
Disabled Person (Services Consultation and Representation) Act 1986. HMSO.
Discipline in Schools: Report of the Committee of Enquiry (1989), (The Elton Report). DES/HMSO.
Education Act 1944. HMSO.
Education Act 1993. HMSO.
Education Reform Act 1988. HMSO.
Education (Special Educational Needs Code of Practice) (Appointed Day) Regulations 1994, SI 1994. HMSO.
SEN Tribunals: Consultative Paper on Draft Regulations and Rules of Procedure. DFE.
SEN Tribunal Regulations 1994, SI 1910. HMSO.
SEN Tribunal: how to appeal. DFE Publications Centre.
Special Educational Needs: a guide for parents, 5/94. DFE Publications Centre.

Hampshire publications

These titles have been published in Hampshire with the Code of Practice in mind and are obtainable from the Education Department Publicity Unit, The Castle, Winchester SO23 8UG.
N1 *A Guide for Schools: The SEN Code of Practice* (Newsheet).
N2 *A Guide for Schools: The Named Person and the SEN Code of Practice* (Newsheet).
L1 *What are Special Educational Needs* (12 page leaflet).
L2 *Your Young Child's Development* (12 page leaflet).
L3 *Autism* (8 page leaflet).
L4 *Portage* (4 page leaflet).
L5 *The Annual Review* (8 page leaflet).
L6 *An Audit of Special Educational Needs* (4 page leaflet).
L7 *Hampshire's Education Service and Parents in Partnership* (4 page leaflet).
L8 *The Named Person (Befriender): A Guide for Parents and Carers* (8 page leaflet).
L9 *Further Statutory Assessments: A Guide for Parents and Carers* (4 page leaflet).

Other publications

(This list comprises titles for further reading and titles referred to in the text)
Advisory Centre for Education (ACE) (1995), *Special Education Handbook*. London.
Advisory Centre for Education (ACE) Publications, *Special Needs – Support for Governors*. London, 1994.
Ainscow, M. (1991), *Effective Schools for All*. London: David Fulton Publishers.
Aldridge, T. (1995), 'Appeal in Progress', *Education*, 5 May.

Barton, L. (1987), *The Politics of Special Educational Needs*. Lewes: Falmer Press.

Booth, T. (1994), 'Continua or chimera', *British Journal of Special Education*, Vol.21, No.1, pp.21–24.

Branston, P. and Provis, M. (1986), *Children and Parents Enjoy Reading*. London: Hodder and Stoughton.

Buckley, S. and Bird, G. (1994), *Meeting the Educational Needs of Children with Down's Syndrome: A Handbook for Teachers*. University of Portsmouth, Hampshire.

Carnall, C. (1989), *Managing Change*. Hemel Hempstead: Prentice Hall.

Chasty, H. and Friel, J. (1991), *Assessment Law and Practice – Caught in the Act*. London: Kingsley.

Cohen, A. and Cohen, L. (eds) (1986), *Special Educational Needs in the Ordinary School*. London: Harper and Row.

Cornwell, N. (1987), *Statementing and the 1981 Education Act*. Bedford: Cranfield Press.

Cronk, K.A. (1987), *Teacher-Pupil Conflict in Secondary Schools*. Lewes: Falmer Press.

Denman, R. and Lunt, I. (1993), 'Getting Your Act Together: Some Implications for EPs of cases of judicial review', *Educational Psychology in Practice*, Vol.9, No.1, pp.9–16.

Denman, R. and Lunt. I. (1995), 'More or Less Appealing Act', *Educational Psychology in Practice*, Vol.10, No.4, pp.238–246.

Galloway D., Armstrong, A. and Tomlinson, S. (1994), *The Assessment of Special Educational Needs: whose problem?* London: Longman.

Galloway, D. (1976), 'Size of school, socio-economic hardship, suspension rate and persistent unjustified absence from school', *British Journal of Educational Psychology*, Vol.46, No.1, pp.40–47

Galloway, D. (1986), in Cohen, A. and Cohen, L. (eds) *Special Educational Needs in the Ordinary School*. London: Harper and Row.

Gersch, I.S. et al (1993), 'Valuing the Child's Perspective: A revised student report and other practical initiatives', *Educational Psychology in Practice*, Vol.9, No.1, pp.36–45.

Hannavy, S. (1995), 'Able and Willing', *Special Children*, May issue.

Ingram, J. and Worrall, N. (1993), *Teacher-Child Partnership*, London: David Fulton Publishers.

Johnson, P. (1995), 'Costing the SEN Code of Practice', *Education*, 26 May.

Lunt, I. and Evans, J. (1994), 'Allocating resources for Special Educational Provision', Policy Options for Special Needs. Stafford, NASEN.

Macbeth, A. (1989), *Involving Parents*, Heinemann Educational.

Peter, M. (1995), 'Trends in law: fifteen years of education policy making, 1979–94' in Potts, P., Armstrong, F. and Masterton, M. (1995), *Equality and Diversity in Education, Vol. 2*. Milton Keynes: Open University.

Potts, P., Armstrong, F. and Masterton, M. (1995), *Equality and Diversity in Education, Vols. 1 and 2*. Milton Keynes: Open University.

Reynolds, D. (1976), 'The Delinquent School' in Hammersley, M. and Woods, P. (eds), op.cit., 58, 85, 93–94.

Reynolds, D. and Murgatroyd, D.S. (1979), 'The Sociology of Schooling and the Absent Pupil: The school as a factor in the generation of truancy' in Carroll, H.C.M. (ed) *Absenteeism in South Wales: Studies of pupils, their homes and their secondary schools*. Swansea: Faculty of Education, University of Swansea.

Robinson, J. (1994), 'Special Educational Needs after the 1993 Reforms', *Education and the Law*, Vol.6, No.1, pp.3–14.

Russell, P. (1994), 'The Code of Practice: New partnerships for children with special educational needs', *British Journal of Special Education*, Vol.21, No.2, pp.48–52.

Rutter, M. and Madge, (1981), *Cycles of Disadvantage*. London: Heinemann.

Rutter, M., Maughan, B., Mortimore, P. and Ouston, J, (1979), *Fifteen Thousand Hours: secondary schools and their effects on children*. London: Open Books.

School Curriculum and Assessment Authority (1994), *Dearing: The Final Report.* London: SCAA.

Scott, L. (1994), *Special Needs: Support for Governors.* Advisory Centre for Education (ACE), June.

Simmons, K. (1994), 'Decoding a new message', *British Journal of Special Education,* Vol.21, No.9, pp.56–59.

Skrtic, T. (1991), in Ainscow, M. *Effective Schools for All.* London: David Fulton Publishers.

Special Children (1995a), 'Tribunal Hit by rush of Appeals', March issue.

Special Children (1995b), 'High Court Case New Blow to Tribunal', April issue.

Times Educational Supplement (1994), 'Lawyers getting ready for big boom in business when Special Needs Tribunals arrive in September'. 25 February.

Tizard, B. and Hughes, M. (1984), *Young Children Learning.* London: Fontana.

Tizard, B., Schofield, W.N. and Hewison, J. (1982), 'Collaboration between Teachers and Parents in assisting children's reading', *British Journal of Educational Psychology,* Vol.52, No.1, pp.1–15.

Topping, K. and Wolfendale, S. (eds) (1985), *Parental Involvement in Children's Reading.* London: Croom Helm.

Vevers, P. (1992), 'Getting in on the Act', *British Journal of Special Education,* Vol.9, No.3, pp.88–91.

Ware, J. (1994), *Educating Children with Profound and Multiple Learning Difficulties.* London: David Fulton Publishers.

Wolfendale, S. (1988), 'The Parental Contribution to Assessment', *Developing Horizons 10.* Available from NCSE, 1 Wood Street, Stratford-upon-Avon.

Wolfendale, S. (ed) (1989), *Parental Involvement: Developing Networks between Home, School and Community.* London: Cassell.

Wolfendale, S. (1992), *Empowering Parents and Teachers.* London: Cassell.

Wright, J. (1994), 'Promises, promises', *Special Children,* 71, pp.11–12.

Wright, J. (1995), 'From Bill to Act: the passing of the 1993 Education Act' in Potts, P., Armstrong, F. and Masterton, M. *Equality and Diversity in Education, Vol.2.* Milton Keynes: Open University.

Index